REDISCOVERING THOMAS C. FLETCHER

The Lost Missouri Governor

Stephen F. Huss, Ph.D.

WESTBOW
PRESS®
A DIVISION OF THOMAS NELSON
& ZONDERVAN

WestBow Press books may be ordered through booksellers or by contacting:

WestBow Press
A Division of Thomas Nelson & Zondervan
1663 Liberty Drive
Bloomington, IN 47403
www.westbowpress.com
1 (866) 928-1240

ISBN: 978-1-9736-4381-4 (sc)
ISBN: 978-1-9736-4382-1 (hc)
ISBN: 978-1-9736-4380-7 (e)

Library of Congress Control Number: 2018912902

Print information available on the last page.

WestBow Press rev. date: 12/19/2018

Dedication

This book is dedicated to the members of The Fletcher House Foundation that have tirelessly and lovingly maintained and enriched the historic first home that Tom and Clara Fletcher lived in; and dedicated to the men and women of the Sons of Union Veterans of the Civil War and Auxiliary to the Sons of Union Veterans of the Civil War—especially to the General Thomas C. Fletcher Camp #47 who carry on the honor traditions of Fletcher's military career and to my grandchildren: Alexandra, Andy, Kirsten, Zachary, Kierra, Ana, Patrick, Charlotte, Madeline, Elliott, Kora, and Emilia in the hopes that they will always search for truth and recognize integrity as they live a meaningful life of service to others.

Contents

Introduction

Although he had been the first Republican Governor in the history of the state, the first native-born governor, the last Civil War governor, the Reconstruction governor, an internationally-respected statesman, the friend of at least five U.S. presidents, and a nationally recognized war hero, most Missourians have never heard of Thomas Clement Fletcher.

To be honest, when I was asked to become a member of the Fletcher House Foundation in 2003, I did not know who he was either. I just thought the quaint little house located just a few blocks from the Jefferson County Court House in Hillsboro appeared to be worth preserving—just because of its historic nature. I joined the small group and began to wonder about the man whose house I now committed myself to care for. Although my "regular job" involved running a mental health center, for twenty-years I had also taught American History as an adjunct at the local community college. This allowed me access to the Jefferson College library. I soon began a cursory review of its available materials to find out more about Thomas C. Fletcher. What I found surprised me; although it probably shouldn't have.

First of all, there are no scholarly biographies written about Thomas Clement Fletcher. The only "book" about him appeared to be more of a "bound pamphlet." It mostly reprinted common material found elsewhere and had no footnotes. The absence of source documentation meant that "leads" to other sources were not available.

Most books that deal with Missouri History merely mention Tom Fletcher's Civil War election and his personal reservations about the notorious "Drake Constitution." Sometimes books would mention that he was the first Republican governor or the first native-born Missourian elected to the office. His signing of the first Emancipation Proclamation by a United States governor frequently merited a line or two. A few very old pamphlets provided local lore about his family, education, and military service but provided no scholarly resources validating these minimal assumptions. At the time, this was enough for me. Clearly, Tom Fletcher had been important to Missouri and probably admirable. He was one of only three governors who lived in Jefferson County. That alone, I decided warranted support for his first personal home. But, I still wondered about Thomas C. Fletcher—who was he, really?

Life interceded. My volunteer work with the foundation unsuccessfully competed with my corporate responsibilities as a C.E.O. until my retirement in 2016. As I looked ahead shortly after my last day at work, my thoughts again turned to Fletcher. By this time, the ownership of the Fletcher House property had been transferred from the Jefferson County government to the City of Hillsboro. The Foundation still funded and maintained the property. But, it had not developed into the "destination site" I thought it might. Of course, I had done little to help.

Before the property could be expanded and improved, funding would have to be generated. Potential donors would need a reason to support the effort—and no one knew anything about Tom Fletcher. This meant that the "lost governor," had to be found. I hoped that his story might catch the attention of Missourians. So, I decided to see what I could find.

Now, with time available to me, I began using my Ph.D.—a research degree. It seemed simple enough. All I had to do was just read through a bunch of books and magazines, review his private papers in the Missouri State Archives, see if there were any old newspaper articles about him and look for colleagues of his day to see what they might have said about him. So, I began finding and then reading through a bunch of books and magazines. Well, I first consulted over a hundred books and magazines that dealt with Missouri history, the Civil War, St. Louis, Guerillas during the war, and other related topics. What a disappointment; they all said about the same things about Fletcher—they provided nothing that I didn't already know after spending a couple of hours in the Jefferson College Library back in 2003.

Okay, I thought. It's time to get serious. A trip to the Missouri State Archives illustrated the fact that one should always call first before committing a full day to travel. Upon arrival, the very helpful archivist told me that the State archives had burned in the early 1900's and almost all of the papers had been destroyed. He provided me with three large binders that had some papers related to Fletcher that had been found in other locations and relocated to the State Archives. Pouring over the records, I found a few things: the list of his gubernatorial appointments, copies of some very interesting correspondence between Fletcher and President Abraham Lincoln, a copy of the Emancipation Proclamation signed by Fletcher, and a couple of private letters. Not much, but enough to stimulate my interest. I still felt pretty depressed as the private papers from after his term of office as governor were also elusive; if they even existed.

For a few months, on and off, I kind of "poked around" other libraries in the St. Louis area and looked on-line in my spare time. Then, in early 2018, I became the historian for the Jefferson County Bicentennial Committee, a sub-group of the Jefferson County Historical and Heritage Society. Part of my responsibilities included informing county citizens about our history; making presentations. The county, would celebrate its organization in 1818 on December 8, 2018 with a major gala. I would be a key-note speaker. I decided to find things that people didn't know about the county; some humorous, some poignant and some fascinating. But first, I had to find the stories or learn about the events. Fletcher's story had to be reprioritized downward in my efforts for a while.

In my subsequent and intense research about Jefferson County to prepare these presentations, I stumbled on a new research tool— *Newspapers.com*. The site boasted *"Newspapers.com is the largest online newspaper archive consisting of 300+ million pages of historical newspapers from 11,100+ newspapers from around the United States and beyond."*

Although only four newspapers (in the beginning) were Missouri ones, I thought it might be a good place to start. And, of all the benefits of the site, the resources were all searchable. One could put in the name, the state, and the date range related to the topic one wanted to review and find the result highlighted in yellow on a newspaper presented on the screen.

Crossing my fingers and paying the required fee, on January 5, 2018, I typed in *Jefferson County, Missouri, 1818-1920*. Remarkably, within a few seconds, I found several newspaper articles that gave an overview of the county and a few others that mentioned the words "Jefferson County" in some article in some newspaper. I took copious notes for the Bicentennial presentations. In about a month, I had more than I needed and began speaking to groups. It didn't take long to bring my thoughts again to Fletcher. So, early one March morning in 2018, I opened my computer and brought up the *Newspaper.com* web site. I typed in *Thomas C. Fletcher, Missouri, 1865-1868*. Within another few seconds I found over a hundred listings for him in the various newspapers. On that first day I sat at my computer for over four hours; totally engrossed in the information. This, I thought, held promise.

I then began researching Fletcher in earnest. One source suggested that his private papers might have been donated to an eastern college. Over the next month, I contacted over two dozen eastern colleges and universities trying to locate his private papers. No luck. I thought I was on the right track when I found that his son graduated from the University of West Virginia—surely this would be the place. I was wrong. I contacted the Smithsonian, the Library of Congress, and the National Archives. No luck. I contacted universities in Missouri. No luck. I began to think that his papers did not exist, had been lost, or were buried in some college or university or maybe stashed in some old attic or barn. The failure to find private papers seemed to doom the creation of a scholarly book. But, I determined to continue research on Fletcher. I spent more and more time looking at newspaper articles published during the latter months of the Civil War and during the rest of Fletcher's term as governor. The information took the top of my head off. It was exciting, exhilarating, and dominated my waking hours for weeks thereafter. Once I felt comfortable that I had exhausted the resources available that related to this time in his life, I began wondering about what he did after he left office. Maybe, I thought, he might have at least a few articles somewhere. I spread my search to the period of time after 1868 up until his death in 1899.

Amazingly, I found a treasure-trove of information—actually, *more* than a treasure trove (*whatever more than that is called*). I eventually began just listing his name and the time-frame I was interested in; leaving out the state. Again, I began to see what he had done as governor, but also who he became later in his life. Wow. I found Information about him no modern Missourian ever knew—unforeseen, surprising, remarkable, enlightening and even spectacular things.

I found that his efforts essentially repaired a war-devastated state and began reconciliation between former rebels and Union supporters. I read that throughout his life he advocated for veterans, Native-American and other minority rights, and for an equitable justice system. I uncovered evidence that he was a frequent guest and well-received in the halls of Congress, State and Federal Courts, the White House, and the U.S. Supreme Court for thirty years after his service as governor of Missouri. And he interacted in these relationships with grace, determination and integrity.

Eventually, I completed a manuscript that I thought would be of great interest to the people of Missouri. I created it through my use of primary sources, contemporary newspapers, historical documents and historical analysis. Of course, the one glaring omission in this research was and is the lack of a comprehensive review of his personal papers. They were never located or even verified that they still exist. The lack of personal papers complicated the analysis of his life and beliefs. However, his celebrity (yes, *national celebrity*) resulted in hundreds of articles in various newspapers across the nation. At times, the papers quoted him verbatim and even the selections of Fletcher-related topics by the respective newspapers often revealed the true nature of the man. Being trained in the "American Studies Approach" to research I pieced together the story of his life. My research would result in a final manuscript of about two hundred and twenty pages—small as history books and biographies go; but still respectable and scholarly in nature. I knew that this work could stimulate other historians in the future to use my work as a skeleton from which they could really flesh-out the grand story. My work could be a catalyst; a first-step. It could also benefit the Fletcher House Foundation with whom I would share any profits from the book's sale.

Proud of this manuscript, all I needed was a publisher. Of course, it would be easy—after all, Fletcher had been an amazing Missourian. Everyone would want to hear his story.

I first approached the University of Missouri Press. They were gracious, complimented my work and writing, and suggested that this was a "good *first step*" in the creation of a story that deserved to be told and wished me luck. A bit discouraged, I reached out to other regional publishers. Polite and encouraging rejections followed. One even, two months after rejecting my submission, sent me another letter encouraging me to continue trying to find a publisher because the work was so promising and engaging. In May, 2018, I received a call from Westbow Press, a Division of Thomas Nelson and Zondervan. A Christian publishing company, in 2015 they had published my book *Where's Jesus: American Christianity in Crisis;* a modest success. They wondered if I had any new work in progress. I told them about the Fletcher biography. A slight pause on the phone occurred. The agent then asked me to send them a copy and they might consider the work although it was a bit out of their comfort zone.

They eventually decided to publish it. They were a bit worried about distribution—due to the limited national appeal of a Missouri topic and the probable lack of interest by most Christian book stores even in Missouri. Through them, however, Barnes and Nobel would carry-it on line and in their stores and it would be available on Amazon.com. For several months, revisions, galley proof reviews, and several rewrites flew back and forth between the publisher and myself. Finally, the biography came out in January, 2019.

This is that book.

The final product should be of interest to Missouri history buffs, fans of biographies, those interested in stories from the late 1800's, and anyone who is interested in politics and government. With some good fortune, many who read this will want to support the further development of the historic site in Jefferson County. It is also hoped that future historians can expand upon this research. I have visions of some enterprising young Ph.D. candidate who will read this book and do what I have not been able to do: locate the lost private papers that will give greater insight into Thomas C. Fletcher. Until then, this will have to do. I hope the reader finds reading the book as compelling as I did in researching and writing it.

Stephen F. Huss, Ph.D.

Early Years

In 1827, the United States seemed poised on the edge of greatness. Short of physical stature but possessing great wisdom, John Quincy Adams steered the nation as president. South Carolina's feisty and racist John C. Calhoun held onto the vice-presidency with determination. Larger than life, John C. Marshall still dominated the United States Supreme Court. War of 1812 hero and strong Democrat John Miller served as governor of Missouri with Fletcher family friend, Daniel Dunklin, who served as lieutenant-governor. The United States found itself relatively free from debt and having few entangling alliances across the world. While the American flag did not fly from sea to sea, it surely looked as if it might someday. Wealth seemed within the grasp of many hard-working and ambitious Americans. Emigrants from Europe were rapidly expanding the population, hoping to gain a share. Especially promising, the newly acquired lands west of the Mississippi River appeared ripe for development.

A national road from Ohio to St. Louis seemed assured for the near future. Missouri seemed the logical starting out point for most looking to improve their respective families' lives or to find adventure in the "*Trans-Mississippi West.*" The industrious farmers of the Appalachians, the cotton growers of the South who needed fresh land, the up and coming small businessmen of the Northeast, and immigrants from Ireland and

England, along with a few Germans, looked at Missouri as a virtual promised land. The young state held great promise to the settlers, their children and their children's children.

Fourth of nine, Thomas Clement Fletcher was born on January 22, 1827. His siblings were Margaret E. (b.1818), John William (b. 1819), Cecelia Adeline (b. 1823), Percy (b.1827). Clementine (b. 1830), Charles Carroll (b. 1830). Josephine (b. 1834), and Ann M (b. *unknown*). Each lived their own stories. All were part of Missouri's history that Tom helped develop.

In the year of Thomas Clement Fletcher's birth, Missouri had just been a state for six years—formed as part of the Missouri Compromise. Slaves were allowed north of its southern border. While Tom's parents, Clement Bell Fletcher and Margaret S. Fletcher (née Byrd) had been slaveholders in Sallsbury, Maryland, they had no slaves when they arrived in Missouri, just before the territory became a state.[1] The Fletchers arrived with a substantial but not exorbitant amount of money and two young children. They may have left their slaves with family in Maryland to be sold at some point or they may have sold them in order to have the financial ability to move westward. Jefferson County had been officially formed on December 8, 1818, shortly before the Fletcher family's arrival. Clement and his young wife were ambitious and industrious and they possessed significant business and interpersonal skills. They purchased land just south of St. Louis near Herculaneum, the temporary Jefferson County seat. The town had been created in 1808 by Moses Austin and S. Hammond. Located at the mouth of Joachim Creek, midway between St. Louis and Ste. Genevieve, it was the shipping point for the lead smelted at Valle's Mines, Richwood's, Old Mines, Potosi, and other locations in Washington County. In Herculaneum, the industry on the site smelted, cast and dropped lead from a shot tower before shipping the finished or semi-finished product to St. Louis and points east. Of particular importance, the town hosted the temporary county seat and only post office in the county until 1837. Clement Fletcher probably purchased

---

[1] A 2018 search of Jefferson County Court Records found in Jefferson College, Hillsboro, Missouri found no listings for slaves by this family.

one-hundred-and-sixty acres available at two dollars an acre, the going rate (*which is about thirty-seven dollars an acre in 2018*)—quite a bargain even then. Like the young nation, the Fletchers were poised for something better—or at least for change. The county they had chosen still held on to its rugged nature; the Fletchers felt up to the task.

Jefferson County began the farthermost eastern boundary of the Ozark foothills. The Crystal Escarpment provided an acutely visible landmark for boats traversing the Mississippi River. Its cliffs guided the Mississippi southward. The land itself was composed of sandstone over limestone, along with copious quantities of Dolomite and some important lead deposits—all covered with a subsoil of red clay. Spring-fed waterways like the Meramec River, Big River, Bellews Creek, and others drained into the Mississippi. They provided the only alluvial farm land which was about sixteen percent of the total acreage. Abundant deer and small animals provided sustenance to the Fletchers and to other early white settlers who also had to deal with the black bears that were frequently encountered.

Native-Americans had lived in the county for over twelve thousand years before the Fletchers. They had migrated there for the same reasons as the Fletchers: to better their lives economically, physically, and spiritually. The indigenous peoples spent time hunting mammoths, availing themselves of the salt resources, fish and copious other game. The wooded hillsides, many caves and rivers provided them with comfortable homes and sustenance. Later, the prosperous Illinois Mississippian settlement (*called* Cahokia *in modern time*) used the area for lumber, hunting, small outpost villages and probably for ceremonial reasons. Delaware, Missouri, Shawnee, and most recently Osage and Ilini, had lived in the county after the decline of the Mississippian culture. Of course, the mammoth and bison were also long gone. And the last Indian conflict had taken place in 1802. The indigenous peoples were almost gone by the time Tom arrived as part of the Fletcher family.

Native-Americans from any tribe seldom wandered across the county by the late 1820's. If seen at all, they would be few in number and treading on old trails leading somewhere else. The mostly broken men and some women with children probably walked quietly holding their heads down, knowing that they were unwelcome strangers in the lands their ancestors had left for them. Few of the new settlers could look upon them with anything but pity. Clement might have given them food or other goods from his stores; he appeared to be that kind of man.

Only a few farms existed in the young county. In 1819, when Tom's father arrived, few roads existed anywhere in the county's 657 square.

Herculaneum shot-tower near the Fletcher Home; Public Domain.

The most important commerce center south of St. Louis lay well over thirty miles to the south. Potosi, county seat of Washington County, provided copious amounts of lead to Missouri entrepreneurs like Moses Austin who had founded Herculaneum. But traveling back and forth proved difficult. Old Osage Indian paths and limited farm roads provided the little communication and commerce routes available. *El Camino Real* (later called *Telegraph Road*) traversed the county from St. Louis toward Potosi and New Madrid in the southern part of the territory. The word *"road"* would have been a generous description as these so-called *"roads"* consisted mostly of cleared land irregularly following old paths. Less than two thousand people lived in Jefferson County at the time. The rugged land promised opportunity, however—if one could withstand the hardships.

Within a few years, however, Clement, had succeeded in several endeavors, particularly mercantile related. He eventually owned seven stores in Illinois and Missouri. Clement also began supporting the dominant Democratic Party shortly after his business began to grow. Things looked pretty good for the Fletcher family. Young Thomas came along and would grow up in an opportune time and place.

After the end of the War with Britain in 1815, the United States had entered into *"The Era of Good Feelings."* Even though the war essentially had been a tie (the Treaty of Ghent established the *status quo ante-bellum*), Andrew Jackson's decisive victory at New Orleans bolstered Americans self-confidence even though it had been won after the war had actually been declared over.[2] By 1815, adventurous Americans like the Fletchers could move westward into the mostly unconquered lands gained from Napoleon Bonaparte through the 1803 Louisiana Purchase. They began doing so in large numbers and with great expectations. St. Louis became the jumping off place—the "Gateway to the West."

At this time, the speed of change further increased across the nation and throughout Missouri. By the time Thomas was five years old in 1832, American Indians no longer owned any land in Missouri, a new Bank of the United States (BUS) opened in St. Louis, and the western fur trade brought wealth and excitement to St. Louis. President Andrew Jackson held firm control of the national government, spoils system and all. But in addition to western economic opportunities, Americans also began to critically look at social issues facing them. Perhaps not quite seeing themselves as the "City on a Hill" of the Puritan days, Americans did look more closely and critically at themselves. What they saw gave rise to new perspectives. *Reform* became the catchword for schools, prisons, mental institutions, personal alcohol consumption (*national per capita consumption of whiskey in the 1830's exceeded seven gallons. Women, children and infants did not usually drink so many men were drinking much more than seven gallons a year*), and traditional family roles. Literature and art blossomed. Religious beliefs were challenged and at least one new uniquely American religion emerged in the 1820's—known as Mormon.

---

[2] Communications were primitive at the time. The Treaty of Ghent (so named for the city in Belgium) signed on December 24, 1814 ended the war. On January 8, 1815 the British attacked New Orleans.

But of all the pressing issues of the time, slavery remained the most entrenched and abhorrent—at least to many Americans. Christian churches frequently divided along North-South lines. Politics continually confronted the *"Peculiar Institution"* every time an area wanted to be admitted to statehood. Abolitionism became a common theme for discussions in homes, bars, and political rallies. The issue of slavery continually reared its ugly head—at least in the Northern free states. Jefferson County allowed slaves, but most did not feel comfortable about it. They were less conflicted about billiard tables—a slave might be taxed at fifty cents a year (*about nine hundred dollars in 2018*) but owning a billiard table would cost twenty-five dollars (*about forty-five thousand dollars in 2018*).

Non-slaveholders, but probably a bit ambivalent about the institution of slavery, the Fletchers and their close friends, the Honeys, dabbled in lead mining, land speculation, small farming and mercantile efforts. None of these endeavors were financially aligned with owning slaves— the "cost benefit" did not exist. John W. Honey supplemented his efforts by being a riverboat captain on *The Maid of Orleans* at sixty dollars a month. His river activities also provided lower transportation costs for his and Clement's merchandise that they offered for sale. Modest success shortly ensued for both families who remained close all their respective lives. According to local lore, the Honey's daughter, Mary Clarissa (Clara) Honey, only a few weeks younger than Thomas, became betrothed to Thomas while still children.[3] This certainly could have been accurate as parents at this time commonly betrothed their children.

Jefferson County had expanded largely due to its proximity to St. Louis. While not directly involved in the fur trade, its produce helped to feed the growing urban center. Its lead works provided a valuable commercial commodity to the rapidly growing industrial development. Its available land gave opportunity to immigrants searching for something better. The new county seat, Hillsboro (*designated on February 8, 1839*) sat on a dependable spring located at the first stopping point between St. Louis and Potosi. Due to difficulties in travel between St. Louis

---

[3] "Life and Times," 2.

and Potosi, the young county seat soon boasted three hotels. Travelers probably really needed a rest. Their bouncing ride over only roughly constructed roads—primarily just scraped out of old trails—provided almost no comfort. Holes, fallen tree-limbs and rockslides delayed passage as travelers often had to clear the roads themselves before continuing on. Hillsboro provided a welcome relief but did not boast a large population and did not incorporate until 1873. But, families did populate the area nearby as it provided a good environment for raising children.

Tom's young life paralleled the young lives of most frontier children of the era. About five years before his death, Fletcher reminisced about his own early life and that of the *"Sturdy Pioneers of Old"* to friends. The memories were published in dozens of newspapers across the nation.

> *When I was a boy I lived among the pioneers in Missouri. They were a fine class of people, all the best people I ever knew. They drove back the Indians, and made bear and deer their meat, as the saying goes. It was before the days of the schoolmaster. Occasionally we had a three months' subscription school but the master was employed more for his physical qualifications to discipline the big boys than for his learning. It was before the days of baseball and football, and the sport that stood at the head of the list was 'gander pulling." The men met at some suitable cross roads store, where eighteen cents per gallon corn whisky was dispensed, and they pooled in $1 each, say twenty of twenty-five of them. That was a big purse in those days. They got the oldest and toughest gander that roamed in the circuit. The feathers were carefully plucked from his neck and the neck was covered with grease and soap. After these preliminaries Mr. Gander was securely tied to the swinging limb of a tree, hanging upside downward. This done the men would mount their horses, a circle was drawn., the master of ceremonies took his place in the center of the ring, whip in hand, and kept every horse on a lively run as the riders tried to catch the gander's neck. The man that succeeded in pulling off the neck raked*

in the pot. If he held on until he was pulled off the horse it counted for the gander and the rider was out. It was a little rough on the fowl, but as a feat of strength and horsemanship it was worth seeing, and the knights of old never put lance in rest or rode in a tournament to greater applause among the spectators than was showered upon them by the throng at a gander pulling. I was once an eye-witness to this strange sport. Of course, it wound up with a dance, and the hero who pulled off the gander's head danced with the prettiest girl. Pretty girls? Your young ladies of today wouldn't have been in it with those rosy cheeked lasses. All the candidates for office were there electioneering. They didn't make many speeches in those days. They set 'em up and mixed about and talked with the boys. Well, that old set is gone now. Their descendants are learned and have modern manners, habits and amusements, but they are not any better in any sense than the sturdy old pioneers, their ancestors.[4]

These whimsical reminiscences aside, Tom Fletcher's early life probably more resembled the lives of most frontier children. Watching a *"gander–pull"* would not likely have occurred until he was a young man or at least older teen. He had more important tasks to accomplish within the family in his youth. But they probably were not as much fun to remember or tell his audiences.

First of all, there were family chores to complete—as appropriate to his age. Everyone worked on a family farm. As a young boy, Tom probably collected eggs, milked cows, cleaned stalls, helped in the garden and performed other tasks assigned by his parents. His sisters assisted with baking, butter churning, meal preparation and house cleaning. The girls would also help with ironing, laundry, sewing, knitting and soap making. His older brothers tended to the cross-cut sawing of timber for sale and use, general farming and ordinary maintenance tasks. The boys would assist in building split rail fences, cultivating fields with hand

---

[4] *Arkansas City Daily Traveler* (Arkansas City, Kansas). October 9, 1894, 8.

tools, daubing friends and neighbors' log homes as well as repairing their own home and outbuildings.[5] They would also flail and winnow wheat, harvest grain, groom cattle, mow grass with a scythe, and work with hand tools and shaving-horses. In season, they would grind corn as needed. The boys also worked in each of the stores owned by their father.

During each day, meal preparation in the Fletcher home occupied much of the females' time. The food usually consisted of items that could be boiled, braised or grilled. Large iron pots hung from iron arms aligned along the sides of the large kitchen fireplace. Others sat on trivets placed directly on or near the fire. From these implements came stews, soups, corn bread, collard greens, peas, biscuits, pies and even some delicacies such as cookies and maybe even peanut brittle. Chickens had to be caught, killed, feathers removed, par-boiled, and then cooked (*often grilled with sage or fried in lard*). Even bringing ham to the table required a great deal of timing, effort, and knowledge. Each member of the family had his or her respective responsibility in this lengthy rendering process. In Jefferson County the older boys likely hunted and fished for the family. As Tom's father owned several mercantile businesses, his family's lifestyle contrasted favorably with others in the county whether it be in regard to food, clothing or shelter. Compared with St. Louis however, the Fletchers still lived on the frontier.

Spare time was precious to the Fletcher family members of all ages. Hard work permeated the days of most frontier families. The children provided important labor that could not be obtained otherwise. Tom learned that people working together could accomplish much. He learned how to work with others; even his brothers and sisters. He probably paid close attention to the expectations of his parents who aptly demonstrated the "*Protestant Work Ethic*." The concepts of "obligation" and "responsibility" appear to have been particularly well learned during his childhood. But, he evidently had time to use his artistic talent.

Obvious to most westerners would have been the beauty of the Jefferson County, Missouri landscape. The rough faces of the Crystal

---

[5] Daubing is the practice of filling the spaces between logs with a mixture of sand, clay, water, straw, lime, and manure to insulate the homes.

Escarpment near his home and the picturesque, formidable Mississippi River punctuated with lush uninhabited islands could have provided him great drawing opportunities. Herculaneum's loading docks offered attractive subjects for the young man. Eagles often perched nearby or soared overhead. Riverboats bobbing on the river also likely caught his eye. He learned to sketch with charcoal and pen and ink. There is no evidence that he ever used oils or watercolors. He became quite good although William Turner or John Constable had little to fear from his competition. Tom's time spent in artistic efforts may also have helped him to learn patience and the importance of skillful observation.

He likely also worked alongside his father and brothers in the mercantile side of the family enterprises located on both sides of the Mississippi River. Even when very young, he could have helped stock the shelves, arrange items in display cases, and clean the floors. Like others along the frontier, the Fletchers participated in community activities. Of primary importance would have been the church. Family attendance at the local Methodist Church probably provided a chance to mingle with others, have fun, learn about religious thought, and maybe help Tom get to know Clarissa. His church had long since declared its opposition to the enslavement of others. But, over and above all his other activities in childhood and adolescence, Tom's young life centered on education.

Young Tom had been named after his great-grandfather, Thomas. He had received an A.B degree in 1710 from Oxford and later served as a minister in Somerset County, Maryland.[6] Tom likely wanted to honor his well-educated namesake. It would have been a lot to live up to. Tom was probably also incredibly inquisitive as a young child; he certainly remained so all of his life. Fletcher graduated from Willard Frissell's elementary subscription school in Jefferson County but that provided only the bare basics.[7] No secondary school existed in the County at the time. Frissell also served as the county superintendent of schools and might have seen the potential in young Tom.[8] Notably, after Fletcher had

---

[6] "Byrd Family History," unpublished by Betty Vinyard, Jefferson County, Missouri, 2007.

[7] "Historical and Biographical Notes," Missouri State Archives, Finding Aid 3.18.

[8] Willard Frizzel's papers, Missouri History Museum Archives, St. Louis.

become governor of Missouri, Frissell enjoyed telling people that he was the *"only one who had ever licked the governor!"*[9] Since no local secondary school existed nearby, the Fletcher boys usually took one of two ferries from Herculaneum across the Mississippi to the subscription school at the Harrisonville Landing in Illinois. Local lore suggests they even rowed a small family boat across the river if they couldn't take the ferry for some

Wood cut of a typical ferry of the type used by Thomas Fletcher and his brothers to cross the Mississippi; Public Domain.

reason. The small settlement consisted of a school, post office, blacksmith, and Tom's father's mercantile store along with a few residences. Madison Miller, a family friend and employee in the store, probably attended the school with the Fletchers. He eventually became one of Thomas' brothers-in-laws.[10]

The simple fact was that few levels of formal education existed in any meaningful manner near his home. This only complicated his educational development; it did not terminate it. Tom's parents encouraged his efforts to learn. Tom needed very little encouragement.

---

[9] Ibid.

[10] Monroeillinoisgenweb.org, "Harrisonville Monroe County, Illinois," extracted from *Combined History of Randolph, Monroe and Perry Counties, Illinois*, (J. L. McDonough & Co., Philadelphia, 1883); the store operated until the flood of 1844.

Education

Tom probably only sporadically attended the secondary school over in Illinois. When winter ice packed the Mississippi, a crossing would have been difficult, at best. Of course, there were a few frigid days when he and his brothers could have walked across the frozen river. Frequent spring flooding also complicated continuity in attendance. And, of course, family needs superseded other interests. When he did attend, he probably received directions from the teacher that would guide his own course of study when back home in Missouri. Many frontier students followed this method. Most of his actual education came from within the family—generally self-study. After chores in the evening the Fletcher children's mother, and maybe their father, could assist the children with reading, writing and arithmetic. Clement surely knew that the better educated his children were, the better their chances for business success. Older siblings might also have helped the younger ones as time allowed. Frontier children often learned that helping others also improved their own knowledge levels and interactive skills.

The dinner table functioned as a round-table discussion forum and could have gotten heated as more controversial issues were brought up. Some of Tom's siblings were almost nine years older than he and had their own issues with which to deal. As all the children aged, they would read more selectively than just using the family *Bible*. Although, this spiritual guide provided the basic reading for all. The morality and classic stories of justice and compassion presented in the *Bible* may have stood out to the Fletchers and could have been reinforced through the local church services. Tom immersed himself in learning; reading everything he could—from wherever he could borrow books. Shakespeare's works were readily available in most population centers of any size; even Herculaneum or Hillsboro. Edgar Allen Poe, Charles Dickins, and Nathaniel Hawthorne's works all represented the more modern views of society and were likely available to him as he reached the teen and young adult years. The fact is, adulthood came early in all frontier communities.

Regardless of formal education, Tom's' inquisitiveness served him well and led him to become a critical thinker as well as to seek personal advancement. He likely listened closely when family friends visited his parents and discussed the issues of the day. Many of his father's friends were local politicians and office-holders. Others were businessmen and farmers who voiced their own concerns about national, state and local issues. By the time Tom had reached the age of seventeen, the nation feared potential conflicts with England in the Northwest territories of Oregon or with Mexico over Texas. The death of Joseph Smith, the Mormon leader, also stimulated controversy over the future of this sect and potential conflicts between them and more mainstream Americans. Alcohol consumption in the nation had reached alarming rates and temperance movements thrived—even in Jefferson County. Economic ups and downs were certainly critical discussion topics to the frontier entrepreneurs. The 1844 presidential election campaigns loomed near. The possible election of the noted Henry Clay whose support for internal roads and business likely appealed to Tom's father and his friends. But, the most devastating issue in 1844, a massive flood of both the Missouri and the Mississippi, directly and negatively affected the Fletchers and Honeys. They lost their profitable mercantile business in Harrisonville, Illinois. For a time, Harrisonville stood under ten feet or so of water and even after the waters receded it never recovered. Clement had to work hard to recuperate from this devastating loss. Discussions around the dinner table probably took a more ominous tone at this time. Clement knew that he had to reaffirm his solvency to his suppliers in St. Louis and elsewhere. This necessitated many business trips to the city.

Tom, as he got older, accompanied his father into St. Louis for many business activities. Evidently as a young adult Tom showed some proclivity for commercial enterprises. He likely had been involved with keeping the account books for family businesses. His father obviously wanted him to experience the dynamics of business in St. Louis and probably enjoyed his company. On these trips, Tom also paid attention to the sights of the busy commercial center; sometimes to his great dismay.

Sometime during his youth, a visit to a St. Louis slave sale instilled in him an antipathy toward the *Peculiar Institution* probably not completely shared with his parents.[11] He and his father might have just been passing the court house located just a few blocks from the river-landing docks on their way to some mercantile

Slave Sale; from *Uncle Tom*" Cabin, 1853; Public Domain.

business. Slave sales were held at the court house at the beginning of each month. Large crowds often gathered to see the latest commodities and to fulfil curiosity even if they had no intention of purchasing. Observing this horrific event must have had a serious impression on him. His religious education on Sundays would have explained the horrors of bondage and he certainly had seen slaves working in Jefferson County. All this, however, probably developed more of an uneasiness within, but likely appeared

---

[11] "Thomas C. Fletcher, Governor of Missouri," *The Ladies' Repository*, (Cincinnati, Ohio), May, 1868, 364, (found mislabeled under 1875 on-line).

"normal" to young Tom. It was, after all, legal and common. In some ways, the real, ugly and oppressive African-American experience would likely have been mostly invisible to him. But, watching human beings sold on the St. Louis Courthouse steps as the crowd leered at black women, made crude jokes, and talked about "breeding stock" must have left a deep scar in his psyche. He may have made some personal resolution at this time. He certainly vigorously opposed slavery and the mistreatment of others for the rest of his life.

Also, in 1844, he began working in the Circuit Clerk's Office in Hillsboro under John S. Brickey. Tom's experience with his father's businesses had prepared him to some extent and the local political leaders respected the Fletchers. Clement also had many business friends, worked with the political leaders and served many customers in Jefferson County. He likely assisted his son in

Hillsboro Court House at the time Fletcher served as County Clerk; Public Domain.

obtaining the entry-level position. Regardless of how Tom obtained his first employment, he eagerly began his public service career. Hillsboro must have been very exciting for the young man.

Hillsboro had been settled in the late 1700s and early 1800s. The two founding families, William Belews and John Huskey (*settled in 1820*) still lived near there in 1844.[12] The small, close community catered mostly to governmental and general legal needs. Only seventeen, Tom Fletcher, had been recognized as bright and capable by many in the Democratic

---

[12] The Huskey family, as of 2017, still lived in the Hillsboro, Missouri, area. The family homestead was moved to the Fletcher Historic Landmark site in Hillsboro and is available for visitation.

Party. This mostly clerical position allowed him to watch the political process and learn about government and the legal system. His office duties included recording land sales and court proceedings—tasks that he performed brilliantly. Within two years the County Clerk appointed him deputy clerk, with a raise in salary. For many, this rapid advancement to a more important job might have locked him in to this career path. Not so, for Tom.

It soon became apparent that the young man would not be satisfied in this job. He wanted and needed greater challenges. So, while working in this prestigious position, he secured an agreement that allowed him to study law with Phillip Cole in his Hillsboro office located just across the street from the court house.[13] Many, if not most aspiring young attorneys, began their respective careers in this manner. They would *"read law"* with some practicing attorney who would invest the time needed to assist the aspirant. In most cases, this kind of *"apprenticeship"* worked for both. Routine, tedious and laborious work could be performed by the *"student,"* leaving the *"teacher"* free to follow more lucrative activities. Eventually, each ambitious young man would pass the bar and become a full-fledged lawyer. Tom dedicated almost all of his spare time to *"reading law."*

The only other non-work activities that occupied his evenings and weekends likely included church and, perhaps courting Clarissa (*now called* Clara). Well, maybe some local political action crept into his spare time. Committee meetings, political clubs, and planning sessions could have been important to him and his career. Even though young men could not vote, they played an important role in the political process in the United States. They performed the labor tasks including the distribution of leaflets, erection and creation of signage, facilitation of communication within the party and running errands. Some of the more capable young men also made speeches and actually had some influence with their elders. Tom soon began making political presentations to the community. Even young women like Clara took significant interest in the pollical process. While they could not vote, even at twenty-one,

---

[13] *Bench and Bar*, St. Louis, KC, Jefferson City, Missouri Historical Society Archives, Reading Room, 282.

women could influence beaus, male family members and friends. Their influence, often moral, did make many young men like Tom think more about contentious issues.

Tom's daily contact with the most important people of the community stimulated his interest in the political arena and gave him positive and extensive exposure. Political leaders knew that for the party to succeed, new voters were needed. *New* meant young men who would turn twenty-one and then exercise the vote. Tom appealed to the party bosses and probably considered as real *"up and comer."* His ability and popular appeal, even at his young age, gave the Democratic Party of Jefferson County a real hope for continued dominance and power (*it didn't work out that way*). Tom proved too independent and ambitious to be held down in local politics. But, that would not keep him from having great fun in the Jefferson County political process as he developed his own code of ethics and laid the groundwork for the future.

Election Day in Jefferson County, like elsewhere on the frontier, had an air of festival about it. On the special day, candidates, their families, office holders, and anyone interested in the proceedings all arrived as soon as they could in Hillsboro with their picnic baskets and whiskey jugs. On each of the four lawns surrounding the courthouse, people gathered to await the announcement of the results from the upstairs windows. Fiddlers had a great time providing music for the assembled crowds who danced, sang and clapped in time with the melodies. Small groups gathered to talk about candidates and issues with quiet voices and sometimes not so quiet. Women compared sewing accomplishments and children made noise as they ran about in the safe surroundings of the town square. Great discussions were held and much laughter ensued throughout the afternoon and late into the evening. From around the county the votes were carried by horseback to the county seat as soon as the respective polls closed. Fletcher found himself right in the middle of all the excitement. As Deputy Clerk and then later as Circuit Clerk his election duties were extensive. He had to arrange for the judges that would oversee the voting, assure the accuracy of the ballots, and generally oversee the entire process. Inside of the courthouse, as the polls closed, Tom assisted in the laborious hand count of each vote for each office and proposition. Sometimes late into the night, democracy worked in this microcosm of the national electorate. Young Tom Fletcher watched and learned. He also respected the process. With all its flaws, he learned that the system worked in his county. He further recognized that his own efforts assisted with that success.

Logically, he became an active member of the local Democratic Party that dominated the county; just like his father. Politics just came naturally to the young man. People liked him and even at this young age, trusted him. Just as he later said, the political actions of these early days were not *"speech-making."* Personal interactions were far more important. A political candidate needed to be a neighbor, a friend and someone who had their best interests in mind. He had to be *"one of them."* The concepts of *morality, duty, trustworthiness* and *dependability* resonated within him. He had grown up with these values so aptly demonstrated within his family and had internalized them.

Young Adulthood

I n 1849, his personal political career really ramped up. The people of Jefferson County elected him Circuit Clerk—just before his twenty-third birthday. In this position, he also served as Recorder of Deeds and County Court Clerk.[14] It was a small county. The position had broad responsibilities at the time; even more than in the modern era. Tom created records and prepared the court dockets. He kept records of county payments. He managed the actual mechanics of trials. He called witnesses, let people know when their hearing or trial would be heard and helped them to understand the nature of the court proceedings. Essentially, he "held their hands" during difficult times and gave his sympathetic shoulder to lean upon as appropriate. Tom also kept accurate records of the County court cases, keeping track of civil, probate, and criminal courts. "*Reading law*" at the time probably assisted his endeavors. Tom also became involved with the distribution of County funds according to agreements, contracts and legal requirements. Further, as if he needed anything else to do, Tom served in many ways as the voice of the Hillsboro court house to the community. And, he handled all these jobs very well. "Service" came easy to him. He served as Circuit Clerk until 1857 when he resigned, possibly almost immediately after being admitted to the Bar.[15]

---

[14] "Life and Times," 1.
[15] Ibid.

During the several years after his election as Circuit Clerk (1849-1857), the relationship with Clara must have fully blossomed. They had a lot in common. Their respective families remained close and strongly supported the match. The two young lovers were bright, inquisitive, and concerned. They probably had significant discussions about the social and political issues surrounding them. Active in her and Tom's church, Clara also participated in social groups including the temperance movement.

Alcohol had been recognized as a real problem on the frontier as well as in the towns and cities across the country. By the late 1840's, the national per-capita consumption of hard-liquor had dropped from seven to about two gallons. The temperance movement had actually been, for the most part, successful. Mostly focused on *"hard-spirits,"* the American temperance movement attempted to get people to limit consumption rather than eliminate it entirely. Some believed that a little alcohol could benefit digestion but drunkenness could destroy families. Women were often told to add water to wine or serve beer or wine instead of "hard liquor" to guests. Many followed these suggestions leading toward moderation in consumption rather than total abstinence. Clara, however, took a hardline: no use at all. Tom did not take quite such a stance. In many temperance groups, there were few complaints about beer drinking. Tom had also joined the temperance movement at the same time Clara became involved. The temperance movement also aligned itself closely with religious and abolitionist principles. Some temperance groups were more organized than others and had strict membership with leaders called *"Worthy Patriarch," "Worthy Associate," "Financial Scribe," "External Sentinel," "External Sentinel,"* and other positions.[16] Although a world-wide movement, the participants of each local society used their experiences working with like-minded people to learn how to address the other *"evils"* in the world—like slavery. Clara and Tom might have gone to some general meetings together as they were often held in churches; probably sometimes in theirs. Tom and Clara paid close attention and learned a lot. Their conversations could have been interesting.

---

[16] *Palmyra Weekly Whig,* (Palmyra, Missouri), May 23, 1850, 2.

The fact is that an enduring love developed between them during these years. Clara, while supporting Tom, also had ideas of her own and a personal sense of responsibility and worth. This served her well throughout her life. She was her own person too; not just a pretty face (*although she was quite attractive with a striking complexion, delicate bones and dark hair*). Like the females of the day she had the traditional skills in cooking, sewing, cleaning, caring for children and, in general, being the center of a family. But, her brain may have been one of the greatest attributes Tom found attractive. Her natural beauty did not hurt either. But, Clara could serve very well as his sounding-board for many issues. They would have had many discussions about "right" and "wrong" due to the national attention on "reform." Of course, slavery still burned the national soul.

These early years brought him into his own personal and philosophical maturity, probably tempered a bit by Clara. Of all the issues of the day, slavery remained the most contentious. Jefferson County's slaveholding populace were vastly outnumbered by non-slaveholders. But slaves did work on the farms of Jefferson County even though few land-holdings were over five hundred acres and only one over one-thousand in 1860. The land did not lend itself well to cotton nor other crops like rice, tobacco, sugar cane or indigo that needed intensive, abundant, and cheap labor. Only about sixteen-percent of the land could support farming of any kind that did not require terracing on the hillsides. Slaves were just not financially viable in the county. Nor, were they very visible. Fletcher did see them run errands, perform hired labor for non-slave holders, and travel from place to place for a variety of reasons. Discretion and fear likely encouraged slaves to, as best as possible, blend in with the surroundings. Discussions about slavery in and around the court house, in bars, and even on the street could have been volatile. Slowly, Tom Fletcher began voicing his concerns about the morality of slavery. At this time, however, he had not formed his full commitment to its abolishment; but, he was close. Certainly, nearby St. Louis provided a tinder-box for such discussions. Fletcher often visited the city for a variety of business and political reasons at the time. The exciting city drew people from all over.

St. Louis had quite a diverse population in the late 1850's. It had grown astronomically between 1840 and 1860; from about twenty thousand to about one-hundred and sixty thousand. Immigrants from Ireland and Germany provided large elements of the rapid growth. The Irish Immigrants had always felt "less than" others and advocated for the downtrodden. Germans were fleeing a series of failed revolutions seeking freedom of speech, labor equality, and responsible government. While there were certainly strong pro-slavery advocates in St. Louis, the antislavery antagonists greatly and loudly outnumbered them. Germans led the vocal opposition through its newspaper, *The Westliche Post.*[17] Many Missourians, while not pro-slavery apparently felt divided and bewildered by four issues. Tom and other Missourians contemplated,

> 1) Could the nation legally take legal property from owners? The thought was that even if abhorrent, slaves were still legal property and protected as such. Tom agreed with this. His study had assured him that the law had to be followed even if it made no sense. The remedy, he felt, included educating the public and changing the law.
>
> 2) If a way to emancipate slaves did evolve, how much would it cost the nation? *The St. Louis Republican* looked closely at the potential cost noting that it would exceed "...*about fifty million dollars* (in taxes: with a value in 2018 of $1,363,828,342); ...*and putting them on the same level socially and politically with the white race.... slavery extinction has been pressed on gradually* [anyway]"[18] Where would the money come from? Tom apparently did not worry about the cost and flirted with the idea of colonization before concluding that the African-American population could assimilate with the general population if given reasonable assistance.

---

[17] The paper began in August, 1857; Joseph Pulitzer and Carl Schurz were associated with it in the 1860s and 1870's

[18] As quoted in *The Glasgow Weekly Times*, (Glasgow, Missouri), July 1, 1858, 2.

3) How can the religious issue be resolved? Christian denominations divided over the issue. Some used the *Bible* to justify slavery; others used it to refute it. Supporters loudly repeated passages which urged the return of runaway slaves to their masters or encouraged slaves to be *"good slaves"* who would get their reward in Heaven. Pro-slavery advocates adamantly reported that the Hebrews had slaves and Jesus had not condemned slavery. Further, they noted, Christians held slaves for over a thousand years. Anti-slavery advocates noted Jesus's story of the "Good Samaritan," which could certainly apply to slaves. But, mostly, the anti-slavery proponents did not take the *Bible* literally and noted that it had been written over a thousand years before for a less complex society. They believed in the concepts espoused by Jesus to *"Do unto others as you would have them do unto you"* and *"love your neighbor as yourself."* Tom's Methodist Church followed the latter. So, did he.

4) What would happen after slaves were free? Would it involve colonization, political and/or social equality, or something else? The Abolitionist movement also splintered as some members wanted to eliminate slavery but still believed in segregation in all other parts of society. Others wanted political and social equality. Tom fell into this latter category of Abolitionist.

Tom listened to all sides in the discussions about slavery but had made up his own mind by the early 1850's. In 1845, Fletcher's church of choice, Methodist, had split over the issue of slavery. The dominant Methodist group in the north looked at slavery as an *"evil;"* the southern group felt it was a *"positive good."* Discussions had reached an impasse by the early 1840's but came to a head by the time Tom Fletcher began his first adult job in the Circuit Clerk's office. No middle ground existed at the time from a moral perspective to him, but legally the immoral institution could not be eliminated. The young idealistic Methodist dealt with this inconsistency as issues relative to slavery arose in the county court system. And, he began to look closely at the neighboring big city, St. Louis. They were also having more and more problems.

St. Louis, itself, still allowed slave sales and even free blacks were limited in their "*freedom.*" Laws restricted locations for their homes, put limitations on business ownership, prohibited black Americans from testifying against a white person, and stopped them from attending school. Free blacks were prohibited to move to Missouri. Few exemptions to this law were allowed as it required legal action by a court of competent jurisdiction—a circuit court. It almost goes without saying, they could not vote or hold any kind of public office. They did, however, die in the many St. Louis cholera epidemics and suffered greatly in poverty. Fletcher knew all of this and seethed inside.

He may have seen a news item in the *Glasgow Weekly Times* in regard to Abolitionism in which slave owners attempted to justify their harsh treatment of slaves. The article reported that in a public meeting, abolitionists were warned to leave. They noted that a "Vigilance Committee" would protect the slaveholders who had to be more "*rigid*" due to the "*false sympathy of the abolitionists.*" [19] Such veiled and not-so-veiled threats complicated the lives of anti-slavery proponents.

Even popular temperance societies like the ones Clara and Thomas belonged to (*Sons of Temperance* and *Daughters of Temperance*) vocally opposed slavery in addition to excessive use of alcoholic beverages. It seemed as if everywhere across the nation this issue challenged the leaders and general population. Missouri newspaper advertisements like the one offering "*One Negro woman named TILDA about thirty-five or six years of age; also one boy named ISAAC, a boy about seven years old; and a boy named GEORGE about five years old, and a boy named CHARLES, about one year old,*" as part of an estate sale likely weighed on Tom's heart. [20] Other social tender of the times included the publication and wide-spread distribution of *Uncle Tom's Cabin*. This controversial tug-at-the-heart book evolved into a traveling play that reached even St. Louis. Of course,

---

[19] Ibid.

[20] *Boon's Lick Times* (Fayette, Missouri), February 4, 1843, 3.

the Dred Scott decision by the U.S. Supreme Court in 1856 essentially made slaves equivalent to tables, chairs and cows. As an idealistic young attorney, Tom may have galvanized his feelings against slavery and been revulsed by the myopic and dangerous decision made by the Supreme Court.

But Fletcher also learned that not all slaves accepted their lot. In addition to *"voting with their feet"* against slavery, some African-Americans went much further in their efforts to survive in a hostile white society. One event in 1845 probably scared many whites and would have made Fletcher wonder more about the future of slavery. On one night in early January, 1845, five local slaves who were "owned" by several different "masters" in Jefferson County came together for unknown reasons. After gathering up their courage, late in the evening they crept up to the house of man named Merrick located near Valle's Mine, just south of Hillsboro. With brutal efficiency, they killed him and burned his house. After just a few days investigators had pieced together enough information to determine the identity of Merrick's killers. The five were quickly arrested and taken to the Hillsboro county jail where Fletcher participated in the arraignment and subsequent legal proceedings.[21] He may also have witnessed their subsequent execution by hanging from gallows located on the grounds on the eastern side of the County Court House. Violence initiated by African-Americans, while not common, did occur in the uneasy relationships between slaves and the white majority in Missouri and across the nation. Most slaves demonstrated their resistance by slowing down work and causing costly *"accidents."* Of course, many ran away. There were also an exorbitant number of unexplained fires on the farms and plantations where slaves worked. The fugitive slave law complicated things but rarely was enforced once a slave had been successful in *"following the drinking gourd"* to freedom.

Fletcher would have read about captured *"runaway slaves"* who would be returned to their respective masters because of the fugitive slave act—providing all costs associated with the capture and holding costs were satisfied. Newspaper ads would warn that without such payment the slave

---

[21] *The Radical* (Bowling Green, Missouri), January 11, 1845.

would be sold on the steps of the St. Louis Courthouse.[22] No thinking person could not have had this issue on his or her mind in ante-bellum Missouri.

Throughout his time as Circuit Clerk, the everyday issues regarding free blacks, slaves, and "*the right thing to do,*" constantly confronted Fletcher. Runaways, crimes committed by or on African-Americans, ownership questions, legacies, estates and so on were normal issues with which he dealt. His sense of morality frequently clashed with legal restrictions on black human beings. A Missouri law restricted even free blacks from most common rights. They were required to present a certificate of citizenship and have a court hearing in order to obtain a license that would allow them to reside and work anywhere in Missouri. One such Jefferson County hearing of the time later drew fire from *The Weekly Caucasian*, an anti-Republican newspaper. It reported that a black man named Hiram R. Revels had received this approval from Fletcher years before Fletcher became Governor.[23] This became "*notorious*" due to the fact that this same Hiram Revels eventually became the very first African-American United States Senator.[24] There is no doubt that Fletcher found his personal values frequently tested. And he felt helpless. While there is no record of Fletcher commenting on the incident with Revels, he likely felt proud of himself when Revels proudly walked on the floor of the U. S. Senate and then took his seat.

The American preoccupation with the issue of slavery moved to the back burner in early 1846. An uneasy truce existed between Mexico and the United States over the southern boundary of the Texas Republic which had recently become a state. The U.S. claimed the Rio Grande as the Texas-Mexico border. Mexico disputed this and claimed the Nueces River, giving them almost thirty percent more of Texas than the inhabitants would allow. The area had been a bone of contention since

---

[22] *Palmyra Weekly Whig* (Palmyra, Missouri), September 16, 1847, 4.

[23] Note: Hiram Revels was only two months younger than Thomas Fletcher. One wonders if Fletcher saw the young man as similar to himself with aspirations, desires and determinism but with only a different color skin. This encounter might have influenced Fletcher in subtle or not so subtle ways.

[24] *The Weekly Caucasian* (Lexington, Missouri), March 5, 1870, 1.

Texas had been admitted to the United States as a slave state in December, 1845. U.S. Federal troops had been sent to the disputed territory in case of an actual military response from Mexico. Tom Fletcher, along with the rest of the nation had likely been drawn up in the discussions about a possible Mexican war. Tensions with England over the Oregon area were also contentious but most believed the most likely real hostilities would begin with Mexico. In April, 1846, Mexican cavalry attacked an American patrol in the disputed territory. They killed twenty-six soldiers and captured the remaining officers and men. This attack led to the expected war. The *St. Louis Republican*, on May 9th, noted, *"WAR WAR; The war has begun in earnest—the enemy is on our soil."*[25] This echoed President John K. Polk's announcement that American blood had been shed on American soil. Freshman U.S. House of Representatives member Abraham Lincoln reportedly asked to be shown the location of that spot. Others like Henry David Thoreau, Charles Sumner and former president John Quincy Adams, among many others also questioned this excuse to attack the nation's southern neighbor. Their protests fell on deaf ears.

Newspapers across the nation called for immediate retaliation and war. President Polk's declaration of war surprised few. St. Louis would be a staging center for the upcoming hostilities due to its strategic location. Colonel Stephen Kearney, of Jefferson Barracks, received orders to take and secure the northernmost Mexican city of Santa Fe. Colonel Robert Campbell, the newly appointed Missouri Inspector General, began recruiting volunteers for the militia that would accompany the famous Kearney. Campbell also provided, at no charge, all the uniforms for the Laclede Rangers volunteer cavalry.[26] Other merchants similarly contributed to the popular cause. Fletcher certainly knew about this endeavor that would be undertaken and likely considered joining the adventure. Not quite twenty years old, his position as Deputy County Clerk in Jefferson County probably prevented his enlistment.

For the next twenty or so months Tom, along with others across the nation, closely followed the progress of the war. The superiority of

---

[25] *Missouri Republican* (St. Louis, Missouri), May 9, 1846, 1.

[26] Stephen Huss, *Take No Advantage*, unpublished Ph.D. Dissertation, St. Louis University (St. Louis, Missouri), 1989, 225-228.

military training and more sophisticated weapons eventually resulted in an American victory. Tom, like other Americans, read the newspapers about battles, causalities, and really did not worry about a possible defeat. The confidence was almost palpable. Many Americans were beginning to think about economic opportunities in the lands to be captured—especially California. The war also provided a training ground for future Civil War leaders like Robert E. Lee, Ulysses S. Grant, George Meade, P.G. T, Beauregard, Jefferson Davis, William T. Sherman, Stonewall Jackson and many others.

In February, 1948, the Mexican war ended. The Treaty of Guadalupe Hidalgo stripped Mexico of most of the territory eventually known as California, New Mexico, Arizona, Utah, Nevada and parts of Wyoming and Colorado. Now, the United States stretched from sea to sea in the culmination of its *"Manifest Destiny."* But the Mexican War also expanded discussions about slavery. The successful campaign and subsequent land acquisition rekindled the issues about the expansion of slavery. *Did the Missouri Compromise still hold true; did it apply to the new territory?* Regardless of these questions, almost all Americans were proud of the outcome and their brave soldiers. Tom, even if concerned about the slavery expansion issues, likely felt great admiration for the soldiers whose efforts had brought about such success.

One thing he didn't question or feel helpless about—his love for Mary Clarissa (Clara) Honey.

After becoming the Jefferson County Circuit Clerk in 1849, Tom improved his meager salary. This allowed the couple to actively begin planning their marriage. One of the first decisions involved where they wanted to live. There were a lot of opportunities. He learned about available land for sale through his contacts in government and business. He also may have begun purchasing land in Jefferson County as a speculative investment. Prices in Jefferson County were low. The area was poised for development due to its growth in population and its strategic location between St. Louis and the iron ore areas in the southern part of Missouri. Land in and around the county seat would have been of great interest to Tom. Clara would also have liked it because of the nearby school and church. As soon as the right opportunity occurred, Fletcher acted. He quickly purchased a choice city lot in Hillsboro. It was located only about two blocks from the Jefferson County Court House. The 401 Elm Street site sat adjacent to the primary city spring, along the stage route to Potosi, near the elementary school, and only a block or so from the Union Church. As soon as he had the available funds, he and his family began construction on the home. While a modest structure, it would serve the needs for a few years. Tom, his brothers and father used local lumber probably cut and processed by them. The actual construction could have easily been completed by Fletchers in their spare time. Clara's family, The Honeys, probably also helped. They planked the roof and covered it with shingles. Exterior planks painted white drew attention to the new building which sat amongst oak and evergreen trees along a small creek. The interior consisted of hand-hewn lumber fastened to the

Tom and Clara Fletcher's first home; located in Hillsboro; Permission Fletcher House Foundation.

floor joists with hand-made nails. It had hand-cut planks on the walls. Local river-rock formed the chimney. The whitewashed hearth would be the heart of the home. Slightly out of square (about ten inches), the structurally sound home mirrored the appearance of many nearby houses. It consisted of a general living area, a separate dining and kitchen space and an upstairs bedroom. A wooden outhouse, placed strategically nearby, completed the structure. Clara continued to add to her "hope chest," aided by friends and family as she awaited her wedding day. Thomas continued to study law and serve as County Clerk. According to some, he and his brother-in- law, Thomas Rankin, also opened a mercantile store in Hillsboro. This would have helped their respective families prosper.[27] He and Clara must have been appalled at the instability of the nation at the time but were convinced that they could weather anything together. They both continued activities in abolitionist-focused organizations, continued their church work and had lively conversations about slavery; and their own future.

The Methodist Episcopal minister, H.N. Watts, married them on April 16, 1851 as friends and family looked on with pride. The couple then settled into their modest new home in Hillsboro.[28] In his role as "Recorder of Deeds," he documented his own marriage in the court house official records. In addition to his work as Circuit Clerk, Fletcher continued studying for the Bar during his early married life. Clara proudly stood right beside him and provided a needed anchor for the family. He passed the bar and became an attorney in 1856.

He almost immediately left the Circuit Clerk's position to concentrate on the law. His first legal efforts centered on guardian ad-litem services and some land related work. His practice quickly began to grow and so did his family. The house proved too small, even with an expansion after the births of Frances Ella and then Edwin Lewis. In 1857 the Fletcher family temporarily moved to St. Louis.[29]

These new personal responsibilities did not prevent his political involvement.

---

[27] Mary Joan Boyer, *Jefferson County, Missouri in Story and Pictures*, Pat Tripp (St. Louis, Missouri) 1958, 91.

[28] "Life and Times," 2.

[29] This home is still in existence and is operated by the Fletcher House Foundation for the City of Hillsboro.

Ante-Bellum

J ust a few months before his marriage, events on the national level both calmed the national political scene and also planted fertile seeds for future confrontation. The discovery of gold in California in 1849 and subsequent exodus to the western promised land resulted in the demand for statehood by the many thousands of new settlers. Almost totally opposed to slavery (few wanted slaves to work the gold fields in competition with white miners), the territory sought admission as a "free" state. Missouri expanded its role as the "Gateway to the West" as emigrants left Kansas City (Missouri), Independence, Westport, and St. Joseph to go to the *land of milk and honey*—and gold.

Until this time an uneasy and largely unspoken agreement had been made that admitted two states at a time—one free and one slave. This kept the balance in the Senate. It worked; well, for the most part. California's petition caused the loose arrangement to unravel. Tom paid particular attention to the issues in California as one of his older brothers, John William (J.W.) Fletcher, attempted to make his fortune in the gold fields by joining the gold rush. The monumental events in California seemed to unleash other concerns laying just below the surface in the nation. They came bubbling up as tensions rapidly and dangerously rose across the country, nowhere more contentiously than in the U. S. Senate. Finally, Illinois Senator Stephen Douglass worked out a deal that, for the moment, resulted in an uneasy calm. The Compromise of 1850 admitted California as a free state. It resolved issues between Texans and New Mexico and had the federal government assume Texas' debt. It allowed Utah and New Mexico to decide for themselves whether or not to allow slavery. It also eliminated the slave trade in the national capital but greatly strengthened and expanded the Fugitive Slave Law that had been on the books but seldom enforced. Unsaid, but in actuality, it discarded the Missouri Compromise and opened the national debate on slavery.

Almost immediately, northern abolitionists and many of the general population grimaced when slave catchers brazenly appeared on the streets of northern cities and forcibly took former slaves into custody. Parents hid their children's eyes as the slavecatchers ensnared their prey right in front of them and dragged them away screaming in terror and begging for help from the helpless bystanders. Thousands of sensationalized accounts of black families being torn apart were published in Northern newspapers in the decade before the Civil War. The American people began to take sides. By the middle of the 1850's uneasy calm began to erode. Divisions ripped apart institutions and families. The Methodist and Baptist Churches had already evolved into northern and southern branches; other churches felt the pressure to take sides. Fletcher's Methodist upbringing continued to reinforce his anti-slavery feelings. He grew more and more strident about the *peculiar institution*. He began to speak out, even to slaveholders in Jefferson County. The success of his legal practice and lucrative land dealings brought him in contact with many like-minded people across the region. In St. Louis, the German community especially appealed to him and him to them. His former Democratic Party did not. Tom began to look for opportunities to support the Abolitionists in the St. Louis area. Clara likely supported his efforts even if they took him away from home and his children more and more as the issues became ever-present and more and more insistent. American political parties also had difficulty dealing with the issue of slavery.

On the national level, Democrats were still important and vibrant. But the Whigs, who were mostly anti-slavery, had slowly faded away or merged with the new American Party. This derivative group mostly supported native-born Americans and were dedicated to the Union. It stood up for religious liberty, free and fair elections, and constitutional law.[30] In Missouri, the sentiments were echoed by F.B. Atwood of Carrollton County when he said, "...*American Party [is kept in this county] by 640 stout American hearts, which represent so many links in that living chain that will bind this Union together, and preserve our American protestant nationality, and preserve the blessings of our American institutions, and bequeath them as a great political heritage to generations yet unborn.*"[31] Tom Fletcher, disillusioned by the Democratic Party which stood for slavery (or at least not against it) in Jefferson County, drifted toward the pro-Union American Party. He overlooked the nativist aspects of the philosophy and initially found the new fledgling Republican Party too strident.

In 1854, the anti-slave Whigs had re-organized into the Republican Party. It rapidly spread across the northern states flying the banner of Abolitionism. Fletcher felt drawn more to local Republican leaders and probably only flirted with the American Party as a whole. The American Party did need young blood and likely latched on to him. He slowly concluded that the party really did not reflect his personal philosophy and distanced himself a bit. He did not renounce their support for the issues he cared about.

As a vocal and very competent young member of the American Party, he began to gain recognition within the state group even without trying. The 1856 Missouri State American Party ticket included Robert Ewing: Governor; William Newland: Lieutenant Governor; Thomas Harris: Secretary of State; J. F. St James: Attorney General; and for Register of Public Lands: Thomas C. Fletcher.[32] Quoting Andrew Jackson's "*The Federal Union, it must be preserved,*" its national convention drafted former president Milliard Fillmore to again run for president.[33] The American Party did not prove successful in this election. They did acquire over

---

[30] *Glasgow Weekly Times*, February 14, 1856, 1.

[31] *Glasgow Weekly Times*, May 8, 1856, 1.

[32] *Glasgow Weekly Times*, May 29, 1856, 3.

[33] *Glasgow Weekly Times*, 1856, 2.

thirty-five percent of the Missouri vote in some races.[34] Fillmore carried Fletcher's home county, Jefferson, by almost seventy percent.[35] Tom likely played a major role in this achievement.

Although Fletcher ran as an American Party member, he did not blindly follow the party ticket. He supported and actually campaigned for the Democrat, Thomas Hart Benton, for governor. Tom accompanied Benton on a whirlwind campaign tour across the state. Benton was an ardent Unionist and opponent to the expansion of slavery although not exactly an abolitionist. His "Independent Democrat" Party (*almost a party of one*) found little support by the pro-slave outstate voters. Even though he was the father-in-law of famous "Pathfinder" John Charles Fremont, Benton did not provide St. Louis support for the famous western explorer. He feared the creation of a "sectional party" as he viewed the Republicans. Such a party, he believed, could destabilize the nation. Fletcher appears to have agreed with him at that time. Because of Benton and Fletcher's mutual interest in the Pacific Railroad construction, they may also have had more contact than just political campaigning. Fletcher spoke highly of Benton for the rest of his life and considered him a mentor. Being a friend of Benton opened doors—politically and economically. Fletcher's actions in actively supporting Benton also gave him experience in reaching the citizenry and running an election campaign. This would later serve him well.

With his tireless efforts and appealing nature, Fletcher had surely been noticed by important people during the 1856 campaign.[36] The St. Louis community remained a relatively small venue. Political and economic leaders all knew each other. They frequently interacted at the courthouse, in the market places, while attending social and political functions and on visits to the state capital. Fletcher surely stood out with his youthful enthusiasm, strong condemnation of slavery and air of confidence. He had attained quite a positive reputation as an extremely capable and honest lawyer. Any political organization would have been fortunate to have him listed on their roles. Membership in political parties by many Americans

---

[34] Presidency, *www.UCSB.EDU,* Election of 1856.

[35] *www.Wikipedia.org,* "Know Nothing."

[36] "Life and Times," 3.

continued to be fluid until well after the civil war. Democrats probably thought they had the inside track with him because of his relationship with Benton, but they were wrong. In 1856, he still had not made up his mind as to which party he would make a final commitment. Even to his friends, his running from office for one party while campaigning for someone from another did not seem that unusual. Fletcher also began even more active involvement with Abolitionist groups in the St. Louis area as he worked on the 1856 campaign. These endeavors were more central to him. They fit his ethical standards. He would speak on behalf of those who could not speak themselves. His presence at rallies and planning meetings with abolitionists did much to solidify his positive reputation in the German community and with others. Although, he did not have a real political "home" yet, by the end of the election season, he had earned an extremely positive persona with many likeminded persons living in the St. Louis area. Republicans, particularly, paid attention the young man and began to court him for the future. Tom listened and quickly drifted to the new political party.

Life continued after his unsuccessful, and unenthusiastic bid for state office. It might be likely to assume that Fletcher could have been happy that he didn't win as his personal and political fortunes turned in other directions. One of the different directions included developing a local Republican Party organization in St. Louis among the German population. He had finally created a political home; one of his own creation. And, he took to it like a duck to water.

In addition to his political activities, family responsibilities and continuing legal studies, Tom served successfully and profitably as a land agent for the Pacific Railroad.[37] The railroad corporation had received State legislature financial assistance since 1851 to develop five trunk lines, one of which reached southward from St. Louis toward Iron Mountain. By 1855 the state, recognizing the need for infrastructure development to assist commerce, had guaranteed over two million dollars in loans to assist the Iron Mountain route.[38] Fletcher and Louis Rankin,

---

[37] "Life and Times," 2.

[38] *Glasgow Weekly Times*, January 8, 1857.

his brother-in-law, between 1854 and 1859 continued to successfully speculate in land just south of Hillsboro laying directly in the path of the proposed railroad line to Pilot Knob and points south. This destination area, called Iron Mountain, contained the purist grade of iron-ore then known in the world. Fletcher and Ranken divided part of their recently purchased land into plats for ease of sale.

By using his influence and personal funds Tom and his friend Louis, Ranken, built a depot for the approaching Iron Mountain Railroad on land the two men owned. This demonstration of support, along with the personal relationship between Tom and his bosses at the Pacific Railroad, encouraged the Railroad to lay its new rail beds just where Tom wanted. Once this became an actuality, Tom and Louis accelerated

THE HISTORIC FLETCHER HOUSE of 600 block North Main in De Soto is being .... Peeples shows that it also belonged for a time to the .... mother.

The Fletcher home in De Soto;
Permission De Soto Historical Society.

their plans to create a town alongside the new depot. With a depot and surrounding supporting commercial ventures, the site quickly obtained a post office. In 1857, Tom's father, Clement, became the first postmaster. In 1859 Tom and Louis' efforts led directly to the creation of the town they eventually named De Soto after the famous Spanish explorer.

Tom and Louis laid out the town with regular plats that almost immediately became very valuable. This venture brought both men some modest wealth for the first time in their respective lives. Fletcher's extended family soon relocated to the fledgling city. J.W Fletcher, his older brother, built the first home in the young town. His father and brothers cast their lots with the city and retained leadership positions for the next thirty years. C.C. Fletcher eventually became the sheriff of the county and a Missouri State Representative. His father eventually ended his work-life after serving as U.S. Postmaster in De Soto. Even Tom's older brother, John William, eventually returned to the city after his adventures out west. The town's many artesian wells also made it an excellent place to live and eventually to provide water for the railroad industry. Later, it would be known by its nickname, "*Fountain City.*" Tom moved his own family there just as the fateful year, 1860, began.[39] He located his house on a small hill west of the planned depot. The beginning of the new decade appeared as if it could be monumental for the Fletchers—and the nation.

By 1860, the Compromise of 1850 had run its course. Many who had voted for the reprieve no longer held a seat in congress. Men less willing to compromise had arisen from the South and from the North. The nation, itself, had seemingly moved on. Many assumed that the nation had nothing to fear and the positive economic climate would continue to boom. In fact, there had been many positive national developments during the almost ten years since the compromise's passage. Hawaii had been acquired. The Gadsden Purchase promised a southern railroad system across the nation. Slave sales and trading had ceased in the U. S. capital. The discovery of vast amounts of gold had rapidly assured California statehood. The Pony Express linked the West to the East; telegraph lines were not far behind. Southern cotton provided the raw materials for English industrialists and the American New England cotton mills. Commodore Perry had opened the ports of Japan bringing an optimism about future economic wealth and prosperity across the seas. American Clipper Ships like the *Flying Cloud* gracefully sailed the oceans in record speeds. The Mississippi River had been crossed by railroads— further expanding the connections and expectations of the country. The first oil well had been drilled; there would be many more in a very short time. And, American literature and art thrived. Hawthorn's *Scarlet Letter* ushered in the decade. Melville followed with *Moby Dick*. Henry David Thoreau electrified the Transcendental Movement followers with *Walden* in 1854. Few literate Americans failed to glorify (and buy) Walt

---

[39] "Life and times," 3.

Whitman's *Leaves of Grass*. American artists focused on the vast natural landscapes which could rival the European castles and Romanesque historical scenes. To Tom Fletcher, the future looked bright—but a dark underside also existed in the nation. Among the books not given much attention by literary critics, was one written by a mediocre writer named Harriet Beecher Stowe. She would expose the dark side of the nation.

The Fugitive Slave Act and subsequent election of 1856 had also divided the nation. Abolitionists had become more vocal and persuasive. The Kansas-Nebraska Act which allowed areas to decide for themselves the question of *"slavery yes"* or *"slavery no"* created a mini-civil war in Kansas complete with atrocities committed by both sides. *"Bleeding Kansas"* applied in reality as well as figuratively. In 1858 the seven Lincoln-Douglas debates for the Senate seat in Illinois galvanized supporters of both views toward the expansion of slavery. Douglas believed that a region could make its own decisions about being a slave state or not regardless of the law—*Popular Sovereignty*. Republican Abraham Lincoln responded by asking him if that meant that *a region can legally keep people out of an area that they have a legal right to be in*? Douglas would antagonize the Southern Democrats if he said yes and the Northern Democrats if he said no. A man of principle, Douglas continued to support his original premise and won the election but lost Southern support for any future ambitions. In these debates Lincoln also sounded an alarm bell when he announced the belief that the nation could not continue half-slave and half-free. Tom likely read the speeches and wondered about this lanky westerner whose name had become anathema to Southerners.

The fight in Kansas became more and more violent, threatening to spread across to other areas—especially into western Missouri where a significant pro-slavery contingent lived. Lawlessness reigned in Kansas even when terrorist John Brown ended his violent anti-slavery efforts on the gallows after an ill-conceived raid on the arsenal at Harper's Ferry, Virginia. But, *John Brown's soul went marching on*.

In 1860, Fletcher found himself right in the middle of a smoldering cauldron of unrest and potential catastrophe in St. Louis. Almost half of the city's residents were Irish or German immigrants or their first-generation children. Half of the state's free population of African-Americans lived there. Their protection had been guaranteed by the Missouri Supreme Court which ruled that free slaves could not be re-enslaved. An uneasy and, one might argue, unsupportive tolerance for the African-Americans existed in St. Louis. The city teemed with all sorts of activity in economic, military, and cultural realms. While limited in manufacturing, the city still provided a distribution point for the American West. Still the fur trading center of the nation, it had diversified into beer production, shoe, and other leather goods manufacturing. Low quality coal-fired furnaces indiscriminately belched caustic smoke across the city. Cholera, measles and yellow-fever still caused church bells to ring daily during death-filled summers. The wealthier inhabitants fled the city for the summer months or at least sent their families away. Regardless, all along the mile-long levee hundreds of steamboats loaded, unloaded, or waited in line to place cotton, hemp, hogsheads of tobacco, piles of bacon, bags of grain, and other boxes of merchandise on the way to merchants. At the north end of the levee steam-boaters visited the bars and red-light districts just under the vision of Lucas Place and the nearby tall church spires.

Politically the state had divided into loosely-defined groups. The Southern Democrats were mainly found outstate and openly supported slavery and secession if need be. Former governor *"Old Pap,"* Sterling Price and 1860 gubernatorial candidate, *"Old Claib,"* Claiborne Jackson (*who did not vocalize these Southern feelings until after his election*), supported this group but kept quiet about their pro-South alignment. They kept close communication with South Carolina, Arkansas, Mississippi and Georgia secessionists. Other Southern sympathizers just loudly proclaimed their allegiance to the South—meaning they were pro-slavery. These outstate, southern sympathizers recognized that with the end of slavery their wealth and, in many cases, their ability to provide a reasonable livelihood for their families would be threatened. They were right. There was no other easy and cheap farm labor in Missouri. Most families had many children but that labor source only went so far. Children would eventually leave home. Reliable non-family farm labor in Missouri proved "iffy" at best. Most common laborers wanted their own farms and were not dependable for the long term. They could move westward or at least thought they could someday. On the Kansas-Missouri state line, cross-border violence frequently occurred. *"Free-state"* advocates confronted *"slavers."* St. Louis residents looked with horror at the bloody terrorism just across and adjacent to their western state line. The Gateway City looked more like an island of moderation floating on a sea of discontent. Invisible, but real, pro-Union walls surrounded the city and minimal parts of the surrounding areas.

By 1860, the few Democratic supporters of Stephen Douglas were mostly irrelevant across the state. Thomas Hart Benton's 1858 death left a Missouri leadership vacuum. Now some of his former Democratic supporters called themselves "Constitutional Unionists." Plagued by lack of leadership these extraneous Democrats had no real home or hope for political office or influence.

Republicans, largely led by local attorney, B. Gratz Brown, and Frank Blair centered their efforts almost totally in St. Louis. Blair, an ardent *"Free-Soiler"* and close friend of the late Thomas Hart Benton, supported abolition but did not go as far as desiring social equality. At this time, his abolitionist views dominated his perspective; that would change after the war. Brown, a cousin of Frank Blair also worked in Blair's downtown St. Louis law office. Brown had served in the Missouri legislature and edited the Thomas Hart Benton newspaper, *The Missouri Democrat.* After swapping insults with a pro-slavery advocate (Thomas C. Reynolds) in 1856, a duel resulted in Brown walking with a slight limp from a bullet to the leg. This did little to deter his fierce anti-slavery position. Fletcher soon became part of the Republican inner-circle with Brown and Blair. Supported by Germans who abhorred slavery, this faction began to mobilize and arm late in 1860 and early 1861. Blair's several hundred boisterous "Wide Awakes" gave a visible military arm to the fledgling Republicans and made people take notice of their commitment to the Union.

While Fletcher had helped organize the anti-slavery party in Missouri in the years between 1856 and 1860, supporters were more of a "movement" rather than a cohesive political party. They did, however, eventually become a significant part of the center of the Republicans.[40] This might have been part of Fletcher's appeal to the Republicans. He had

---

[40] Lincoln University Archives, Founding documents, 4.

an uncanny ability to draw people to him and an infectious enthusiasm. The new mainstream Republicans, as a whole, were mostly abolitionists but were unanimously pro-Union. Fletcher fit in well and showed great promise.

A small group of people were disgusted with all the political parties but mostly leaned toward pro-Union perspectives. Robert Campbell, a famous Irish mountain man turned St. Louis entrepreneur, was typical of these. Campbell, a close friend of Blair, worked closely with Fletcher in matters regarding the Pacific Railroad and supported Brown, Blair and Fletcher's pro-Union positions as did many of Campbell's friends. People who traveled in circles with Campbell, often had business ties across the Midwest and frequently had family living north and south of the Ohio river. They might accept or not accept the morality of slavery but were passionately interested in keeping the nation intact. Many Irish Missourians fell into this category although their attitude toward slavery usually tended to be extremely negative.

After the election of 1856 and the Dred Scot decision, Tom Fletcher's migration to the Republican Party reflected the actions of most former American Party members. As early as March, 1860, Tom actively participated with Frank Blair and B. Gratz Brown in planning Republican state activities and developing strategies for the future.[41] Tom often met with them in Blair's office in St. Louis but also went to Jefferson City for meetings. At the March Republican Convention in Jefferson City, Tom became one of the ten members who would determine the delegates to the national convention and lead the effort to create a state *"Republican Ticket"* for Missouri.[42] In the summer of 1860, Fletcher's strong position in the party had been recognized by the Republican Central Committee. They placed his name on the state ballot as a candidate for *"Register."*[43] Their candidate for governor, James Gardenhire, as well as the rest of the ticket appeared not to really even consider victory at the poll. They apparently used the effort to gain publicity for the new party and to act as

---

[41] Missouri State Archives, Finding Aid 3.18.

[42] *St. Joseph Free Weekly Democrat*, March 17, 1860, 2.

[43] *Glasgow Weekly Times*, July 12, 1860, 3.

a trial run for the future. By this time, Tom's flirtation with the American Party had completely ended.

By the fall of 1860, Fletcher had deeply ingratiated himself with the Missouri Republican Party. He had finally made a commitment—and found a home in the new party. It did not take much time for him to emerge as one of the top leaders in the group. In this role, he continually advocated for the national efforts to the eliminate slavery. While there were some less sure of where this might lead if attained, most Republicans knew it would be the central focus of the upcoming national election. For months Tom and his new compatriots worked on their election plans and party platform. Meeting in Jefferson City and St. Louis, the small leadership selected the members who would go to the national convention and represent the Missouri Republican Party. Of course, Tom would be one of the chosen. He traveled with his friend, Frank Blair, and others in the state leadership to a make-shift temporary building called the Wigwam, in Chicago. Serving as a Missouri delegate to the national convention, he represented the seventh district along with James Lindsay from Ironton.[44] This experience would change his life, although at the time, he probably was unaware of that.

At the convention, Tom's group advocated the elimination of slavery, the retention of the current immigration regulations, one hundred and sixty-acre homesteads for anyone wanting to move into western public lands, the construction of a transcontinental railroad across the central route near Pike's Peak, and the consideration of *"negro colonization."*[45] The issue of secession did not get addressed. But the seeds of the Radical Republicanism had been planted. Fletcher likely wanted additional efforts to bring African-Americans to a state of equality but realized the time had not come—yet.

The convention itself provided a free-for-all, no-holds-bared, old-fashioned political brawl. The favorite appeared to be William Seward (*an outspoken abolitionist and former governor and Senator from New York*). There were others vying for the mantle of the party including the

---

[44] *Glasgow Weekly Times*, March 22, 1860,1.

[45] "Fletcher," *Ladies' Repository*, (Cincinnati, Ohio) 1865. 364.

"rail-splitter" from Illinois. Missouri's eighteen of the four-hundred and sixty-six votes would not be the pivotal ballots, but their voices would be heard. Of course, having several hundred Wide-Awakes dressed in quasi-military garb marching around carrying drums they incessantly banged upon, blowing shrill trumpets and carrying colorful banners would draw attention to Blair—and Fletcher. While the Missouri Delegation did not play the most significant role in the convention intrigue, it did support the "*Western candidate*," Abraham Lincoln. Fletcher appears to have been an early vocal supporter of Lincoln and became recognized as such. The inner circle around Lincoln surely learned about this young man and appreciated his efforts. Later, this would be important once Fletcher ran for governor of Missouri. As the convention ended, this may have been when he began a personal relationship with Lincoln and his inner circle.

The Civil War Begins

T he November, 1860, election boiled the cauldron over.
Abraham Lincoln's victory proved to be the last straw for the
slave states. Southern states, like dominoes, fell into secession
one by one. South Carolina, of course, lowered the American Flag first.
Fletcher, like other Americans just held his breath and waited....

Lincoln carried St. Louis but lost everywhere else across the state.
In almost ten percent of the counties he received one or less votes.[46]
Ninety-eight percent of St. Louis voted against ultra-Southern positions
and supporters.[47] In Fletcher's home county, Jefferson, over two thirds
of the 1,213 voters strongly supported pro-Union candidates Stephen
Douglass and Constitutional Unionist John Bell. Pro-south candidate
John Breckinridge received only one-hundred fifty-five votes but Lincoln
received six fewer than Breckinridge.[48]

St. Louis learned of South Carolina's secession only a few weeks
after the election. A dismal Christmas season ensued. Fletcher spent the
season with his family in De Soto and probably kept in constant contact
with his St. Louis city friends.

---

[46] *Liberty Tribune* (Liberty, Missouri), December 14, 1860, 1.

[47] James Neal Primm, *Lion of the Valley*, Pruett Publishing Company, Boulder,
Colorado, 1981, 244-246.

[48] *Liberty Tribune* (Liberty, Missouri), December 14, 1860, 1.

In January, 1861, things began heating up in St. Louis. The scheduled slave sale for the first day of the month seemed just a normal occurrence. But, the restless, unfriendly crowd seemed different from those who usually came to "improve their stock." Murmurs were heard in the milling assemblage voicing disparaging comments about the upcoming sale. The auctioneer brought out the first group and the crowd began to be more vocal. The angry observers confronted the auctioneer with threats and catcalls. The anti-slave mob began to shout the legitimate purchasers down as the court house steps became more and more crowded with angry abolitionists. The auctioneer and his partners soon realized the sale would not be possible. In fact, this was the last attempt to hold a slave sale in St. Louis.[49] Abolitionists finally stood up and made themselves heard. Charleston, South Carolina might be gearing up to defend slavery but in St. Louis the *peculiar institution* appeared to be on the way out. Tom Fletcher would have learned about this event soon after its occurrence and likely swelled with pride. As with many St. Louisians, Tom knew that he lived in a time where the issue of slavery could and likely would, be resolved—one way or another.

The State Legislature met on January 3, 1861, with the outgoing governor Robert Marcellus Stewart loudly opposing secession. The newly elected governor, Claiborne Jackson, finally spoke up, "*The destiny of the slaveholding States of this Union is one and the same...Missouri will not be found to shrink from the duty...to stand by the South.*"[50] The legislature decided to hold a convention to determine the momentous decision of secession. On January fourth, President Buchanan declared a day of "National Humiliation, Fasting and Prayer." Few in St. Louis listened. Being an active Methodist, Tom Fletcher might have.

Missouri divided further after New Year's Day, 1861. "*Immediate Secessionists*" favored joining the other states that declared against the Federal government and were becoming more vocal. "*Conditional Unionists*" opposed coercion of the seceding States. Unconditional

---

[49] *Lion of the Valley*, 246.

[50] Duane G. Meyer, *The Heritage of Missouri*, (River City Publishers, Ltd., St. Louis, Missouri, 1982), 345.

Unionists supported the "Whole Union."[51] They all feared the future and what would happen to Missouri. Tom Fletcher stood firmly on the side of the Union and against slavery. While continuing his legal practice and work for the Pacific Railroad, he actively participated in the Republican party planning meetings and local anti-slavery events. He may have attended a Union Meeting held in St. Louis on January 12 on behalf of which Robert Campbell sent a petition to Senator J.J. Crittenden. It urged the Federal government to "*withhold and stay the arm of military power, and on no pretext whatever to bring on the nation the horrors of civil war*" and further entreated the upcoming convention to *...protect the Union of the States and the rights and authority of this State under the Constitution.*"[52] Kentucky Senator Crittenden had proposed a series of compromises to the U. S. Senate designed to avert civil war. St. Louis Unionists wanted him to be aware of their support through this petition. Calmer heads did not prevail and his proposals were summarily dismissed by his fellow legislators.

The situation remained volatile. Just before the scheduled constitutional convention, Fletcher probably read the petition "*To the People of St. Louis*" signed by a large number of influential city leaders that encouraged people to be reasonable, patriotic, and prudent in the upcoming convention.

> *To the People of St Louis;*
>
> *We undersigned citizens of St Louis being largely interested in its welfare, proud of its prosperity, and jealous of its honor, feel that the time has come when every principle of patriotism, of self-interest and self-preservation calls upon the people to take the management of public affairs into their own hands.*
>
> *The preservation of the government of the United States, is at this time, the great question, not only of this continent, but of the civilized world. This nation lately so happy, so powerful and so free is now threatened with obliteration from*

---

[51] Primm, *Lion of the Valley*, 246.

[52] Robert Campbell to J.J. Crittenden, January 14, 1861, Letterbook, MLA.

the map of the world, and its inhabitants are filled with
alarm and disarray.

In this great crisis it is peculiarly important that the
Union Men of St Louis and Missouri should speak out with
one voice in tones of fraternity, peace and patriotism.

We believe the people of Missouri almost unanimously
prefer being the Great Neutral State of a first-rate Power
rather than the battle ground between two hostile sections,
always coveted by both and alternately devastated by each
of them.

On this solemn occasion, we earnestly entreat you to lay
aside for the present, all hasty creeds, to yield all personal
aims and desires and to cooperate heart and soul, in the
defense of the Union and the preservation of our rights. And
to this end, we suggest that you (the people) take measures
to bring out for the approaching State Convention a ticket
composed of men of tried prudence and patriotism who
will truly represent the Union sentiment of this City and
County and in whose support all those who under existing
circumstances and devotedly for the Union can unite.[53]

On February 18th, 1861, ninety-six delegates attended the legislative-ordered special convention held in Jefferson City. On February 28th, they elected Sterling Price as chairman of the meeting. But, strongly pro-Union Hamilton R. Gamble had the greatest influence over the proceedings. Gamble, a slave owner, had supported colonization efforts for African-Americans to Libya and had served as the Chief Justice of the Missouri Supreme Court. In that position, he dissented in the Missouri Supreme Court Decision in the Dred Scott case that overturned the *"once free, always free"* Missouri Statutes. Outgoing Governor Stewart argued that Missouri had been purchased by the U.S. government and therefore had no right to secede.[54] The issue of secession resulted in angry

---

[53] Petition, Civil War Collection MOHis.
[54] Thomas L. Snead, *The Fight for Missouri*, (Charles Scribner's Sons: New York, 1886), 12.

retorts among the group. Compromises were proposed; participants were hard to contain. The meeting, after contentious discussions moved to the Mercantile Library in St. Louis in early March. The long, narrow reading room with its high windows and dark wooden walls reflected the solemnity of the occasion.

The reassembled group finally strongly asserted loyalty to the Federal government by a vote of ninety-eight to one (*this occurred although many still supported slavery*). They announced *"...that at present there is no adequate cause to impel Missouri to dissolve her connection with the Federal Union, but on the contrary, she will labor for such an adjustment of existing troubles as will secure the peace, as well as the rights and equality of all the States."*[55]

The group adjourned on March 21 pledging to meet again in December, 1861. Before closing, they appointed a special committee that could call the convention back in session if an emergency arose.[56] While Fletcher had not attended, he certainly read about the events. And, his friends who attended would have certainly discussed the results with him and others. He might even have been encouraged; but that faint glimmer of hope for national sanity would not have lasted very long.

The new governor, Claiborne F. Jackson, *"loved the Union, but not with the love with which he loved Missouri...nor as he loved the South where he was born and where his kindred lived,"* later wrote Thomas Snead who had served with the governor as Acting Adjutant-General of the State Guard.[57] Governor Jackson, almost immediately after being sworn in, initiated a political take-over of the St. Louis Police Department to thwart the "Wide Awakes." He appointed former governor, Sterling Price, to head the State Guard. Jackson also began urgent correspondence with Confederacy leaders. On March 2, 1861, the governor had announced that even though the Federal supporters had a significant majority against secession that

---

[55] *http://gathkinsons.net/sesqui/?p-2265*, Gathman, Allen "March 19, 1861: Missouri Convention rejects secession," March 19, 2011.

[56] William E. Parrish, *A History of Missouri, Vol. III*, University of Missouri Press, 2001, 30.

[57] Ibid., 19.

I stand here today, come weal, come woe, sink or swim,
survive or perish, to cast my political fortunes foe all time, to
give all that I have, and all that I am, to that people which
is mine by lineage, by birth, and by institutions—the people
of the South…. (the Republicans must cease oppressing the
seceded States) or in the red glare of battle, and in the shock
of contending armies, we will appeal to the God of Battles,
and ask Him to protect us.[58]

He paid great attention to the fact that in many southern states federal arsenals had been surrendered to the state authority—often at the point of a bayonet.[59] Fletcher and his fellow Missourians again held their breath, just waiting until something happened somewhere—just a matter of time.

Far to the east, Major Robert Anderson commanded the federal troops that had evacuated to Fort Sumter located in the middle of the harbor of Charleston, South Carolina on December 26th. Anderson, an expert in artillery, had distinguished himself during the Mexican-American War. His expertise had been recognized with a promotion to Major. Eventually he taught at West Point before being posted to Charleston. The unstable situation in Charleston led him to question his ability to hold on to Federal property in the city. He decided to remove his troops to a more defendable position. Anderson finally removed his indefensible headquarters on the coast just six days after South Carolina seceded. He took over Fort Sumter. This unfinished fort, located in the middle of the harbor, would have to regularly supplied and eventually be reinforced by Washington D.C., but it presented a visible federal presence. As long as the American flag flew, the harbor still belonged to the nation. Across the harbor, the rebels looked on the Federal held fort as an insult. Tom Fletcher had probably never heard of this fort—that would change for him and the rest of the nation.

At 4:30 am on April 12, 1861, Major Anderson awakened to incoming

---

[58] Ibid., 70-71.
[59] Ibid., 36.

iron shot from Confederate shore batteries. Bugles immediately called the defenders to the walls. P.G.T. Beauregard's Confederate artillery battery leveled continuous fire at the stronghold as the American Flag flew over Fort Sumter for the rest of the day. Beauregard had been Major Robert Anderson's student at West Point. The irony may not have been much on Anderson's mind. About two o'clock in the afternoon, on April 13th, only thirty-two hours later, Anderson lowered the thirty-three-star American flag and surrendered his command. The flag was folded and retained by Anderson.[60] With permission from the victorious rebels, he then withdrew to Washington, D. C. as his victorious adversaries waved their hats, jumped up and down and yelled "*Huzzah!*" *Alea iactia est*, Tom Fletcher might have thought to himself when he learned of the disaster.

Once Fort Sumter had fallen, President Abraham Lincoln requested troops from northern states; including four Missouri Regiments. Governor Jackson refused with a terse response, "*Your requisition, in my judgment, is illegal, unconstitutional, and revolutionary in its objects, inhuman and diabolical and cannot be complied with.*"[61] The governor then sent state guard troops to various locations across the state for "training exercises."[62]

---

[60] In 1865, Major Anderson (by then *General* Anderson) returned to Fort Sumter after Lee's surrender. He then raised the same flag that he had lowered at the beginning of the war.

[61] Meyer, *Heritage of Missouri*, 351.

[62] Snead, *The Fight for Missouri*, 151-3.

St Louis, Early in the War

J ust a little over two weeks later, about eight hundred men loyal to the Southern cause, under General Daniel M. Frost, arrived in St. Louis. In 1858, Frost had been appointed Brigadier General of Missouri Volunteer Militia by the former governor, Robert Marcellus Stewart. A hero of the Mexican War and Indian wars, his allegiance to the expansion of slavery and vocal support for slave-holding plantation-owners also stood out in his career. Frost soon camped on high ground located less than two miles from the St. Louis Arsenal and Laclede's landing near the edge of the city (near the junction of modern day Grand and Olive Streets). Frost had encouraged Governor Jackson in the planning of this endeavor and proceeded to carry out the plan. The federal arsenal at Liberty, Missouri, had already surrendered without a shot. After the arrival in St. Louis of several cannon sent by Confederate President Jefferson Davis, the officers of the Frost Militia at "Camp Jackson," began making final plans for taking the arsenal. They needed to assure the control of St. Louis and the Mississippi River. The city controlled the destiny of Missouri with its strategic position. The thousands of stockpiled weapons were needed to assist the pro-South Missouri military.

Not only St. Louis, but Missouri, itself, lay geographically in a strategic position. Communication and travel west were anchored in Missouri. Three major waterways either went through the state or touched it: Mississippi, Missouri, and Ohio. The state provided great amounts of agricultural produce and ranked eighth in population in the nation. The loss of the state could endanger Illinois, Kansas, Iowa and the entire western region. For the forces of the Union, it had to be secure. For the South, the state needed to provide the war material, manpower and support it needed. The South had already added a Missouri star on its battle flag. Frost probably flew this flag over "Camp Jackson." Of course, the American flag had no presence.

Of particular importance to the Union were the German supporters residing throughout the St. Louis area. Fletcher frequently met with them on political matters and many of his German friends lived in the northern part of Jefferson County. Eventually, over thirty-thousand Germans from across the nation enlisted in the Northern Army. Most of these immigrants had left the German city states, especially after the revolution of 1848 and 1849. They sought to avoid the totalitarian and conservative, repressive governments who had successfully retained control over various city-states and regions. The immigrant Germans were fiercely anti-slavery. They felt themselves to have been essentially enslaved by the aristocrats of Europe. However, two-thirds of the general Missouri population had their roots in southern states and looked at the Germans with disdain. Fletcher's own Southern roots had not prevented him from becoming friends with the most powerful German in St. Louis, Frank Blair. Their warm relationship continued as the nation quaked.

Frank Blair's Wide Awakes, the primarily German quasi-military force he had been nurturing for the Chicago Republican Convention protection and paraded them so successfully, now became core of the "Home Guard." They functioned under the command of Blair and later were assimilated into the regular army under Nathaniel Lyon. They had a great deal of support from the St. Louis community. Robert Campbell provided, at no cost, the blue cloth which would clothe the entire regiment when it was enrolled into the Northern army. Blair perceived Jackson's thinly veiled attempt to secure Federal arms by the Confederacy and take the arsenal. Blair used his political influence to have the Federal Commander of the arsenal, General William Selby Harney, whom he did not trust, called away.[63] Political pressure soon ended Harney's command in St. Louis. Captain Nathaniel Lyon took temporary command of the remaining military forces at the arsenal. He quickly posted companies to defend the various approaches to the arsenal. A West Point graduate and veteran of the war with Mexico and Indian wars, Lyon quickly became a close friend of Frank Blair and colleague of Tom Fletcher.

Lyon, almost immediately upon taking command and before the arrival of Frost, secretly removed surplus munitions and arms from the Arsenal to prevent their use by the governor should the arsenal fall. Rebel spies and supporters had not learned this.

On May 10th, just a few days after Frost's arrival in St. Louis, almost ten thousand regular and militia forces surrounded "Camp Jackson" and forced a surrender.[64] According to folk lore passed down through the ages, Lyon had his suspicions about the "training" exercises that were taking place at the site but needed proof. In order to find out for sure, he allegedly dressed up as a woman in a long dress, placed two revolvers under a lap-blanket and drove a buggy through "Camp Jackson." He drove slowly, paying attention to the men milling about and talking in loud voices. Overhearing pro-South, anti-Union pronouncements, watching Confederate flags rustle in the breeze, observing rough cut street signs named "Jefferson Davis Blvd," "Confederacy Ave," and so, on convinced him of the nefarious intent of the group. Probably seeing several limbered cannons also gave him pause.

It is likely that Fletcher would have known if this account accurately described real reconnaissance; there are no records that he ever repeated it. There are no records either of anyone saying that Lyon had not done this. Regardless, the troops did force the surrender of Frost's encampment without firing a single shot.

---

[63] General Harney, while a Tennessean, appeared to be pro-Union but not Anti-South. This got him in trouble with the Blair faction. Harney eventually served in Washington D. C. in administrative positions but never took a field command.

[64] Some accounts suggest the Federal troops numbered closer to seven thousand; it was enough to force the surrender.

They liberated

> *three thirty-two pounders. Three mortar beds. A large*
> *quantity of balls and bombs in ale barrels. Artillery pieces in*
> *boxes labelled 'Tamaroa, care of Greely & Gale, St. Louis—*
> *Iron Mountain Railroad.' Twelve-hundred-hundred rifles*
> *of late mode.... Six field pieces of brass. Twenty-five kegs*
> *of powder. Ninety-six ten-inch bomb shells... Six brass*
> *mortars.... five boxes of canister shot, each box containing*
> *fourteen shot— Fifty artillery swords... several chests of new*
> *muskets. Large number of musket stocks and musket barrels,*
> *separate from each other, all new.*[65]

Lyon quickly moved the prisoners to Olive Street and paused trying to determine his next steps. A short time passed and then they began marching toward the Arsenal. As Federal forces marched their captives eastward, an unruly mob yelled insults, threw rocks and then someone fired a pistol. As with "*The Shot Heard 'Round the World*," fired at Lexington bridge in 1775, the origin of this shot became the topic of history and folk history. "*A drunk fired the shot." "A cowardly German fired it." "Someone in an alley fired it and had nothing to do with the prisoners." "Blair ordered it.*" And, so on....

Regardless of the source, the untrained militia opened fire killing over two dozen people including a child.[66] Among those in the nearby crowd were Ulysses Grant and William T. Sherman, both future U.S. notable generals.

Only a few days later, all prisoners were processed and their weapons removed. They were paroled and told to go home and never again take arms against the Union. They went home but most ignored their pledges. Frost almost immediately after his release began interacting with Jackson and Price. They began recruiting volunteers as part of the Missouri State

---

[65] *Glasgow Weekly Times*, May 16, 1861, 2.

[66] Ibid., 353-355; *www.Pricecamp.org*.

Guard to oppose the Federal forces and take over the state.[67] Union-oriented Home Guards in St. Louis County likewise began to meet on a regular basis in order to prepare for the worst.[68] Both sides were now armed and conflict almost assured.

As these events progressed, Fletcher still resided in De Soto but conversed with many friends among the power structure of St. Louis. He traveled to the city via the Iron Mountain Railroad for which he still provided legal representation. By the end of May, 1861, General Harney had been permanently removed and Captain Lyon promoted to Brigadier General with command of the troops in and around St. Louis. In the middle of June, Governor Jackson and Sterling Price met with General Lyon and Frank Blair at the Planter's House to reach some accord that might prevent actual armed conflict. For about five hours they tried to avoid hostilities but could reach no common accord. Lyon finally ended the conversation and sealed the inevitability of military action as he reportedly told Jackson and Price, "...*This means war. In one hour one of my officers will call for you and conduct you out of my lines.*"[69]

Jackson and Price hurried back to Jefferson City, carted up the state treasury, important papers, gathered together their supporters and moved away from their supposed pursuers. Fletcher began wrapping up his personal legal business or turned it over to others and told his real-estate partner, Louis Ranken, of his own plans. Fletcher had a sound financial position and his family would be okay regardless of his absence. Profitable land deals had enriched him and as long as the property held its value, Fletcher had the ability to do what he wanted. He wanted—*he* need*ed*—to be part of the approaching momentous calamity.

Fletcher wanted to fight for abolition. There would be no way he could avoid service and still be at peace with himself. In some ways, his entire life

---

[67] St. Louis University, at the request of Frost's daughter and a gift of about a million dollars named its main campus *"Frost Campus."* The campus includes the former site of Camp Jackson. In 1887, Frost invited Fletcher, then the chairman of War Governors, and his fellow governors to a dinner at his home at 1711 Carr Place in St. Louis in appreciation for Fletcher and his fellow governors who had done "their duty."

[68] *Republican*, May 5, 1861, 1

[69] Meyer, *Heritage*, 355-357; Snead, *Fight for Missouri*, 200.

prepared him for this moment. Duty, responsibility, determination; these values that he treasured, assured his active participation in the upcoming war. He had no illusions about the war being fought for "*States Rights*;" slavery was the issue. And, he would help end this abomination. Likely Clara understood and supported his decision; although surely with great dread. He enlisted with a rank of first lieutenant. General Lyon, probably at the request of Frank Blair, appointed him assistant provost-marshal general with headquarters in St. Louis. Blair and Fletcher were friends and their political and social attitudes continued in alignment. Eager to be a part of this crusade, Fletcher entered his new position with zeal and confidence. This position also allowed him to remain actively involved with the local Republican Party leadership.

In his new position, Fletcher dealt with military matters, discipline measures such as drunkenness and gambling, military/civilian controversies, refugee problems, and general legal matters that involved any military situation in St. Louis. Lyon soon left the city to follow and engage Jackson and Price. Fletcher continued with his military responsibilities and became ingrained as part of the "up and comers" of the day both militarily and politically. He would never see Lyon again. Badly wounded and still on horseback leading the final charge at Wilson's Creek in August, 1861, Lyon fell dead after sustaining at least three Confederate rifle shots. Price and Frost retreated into Arkansas toward Pea Ridge. Lyon had been the first Northern General killed in the Civil War; there would be many more.

In July, 1861, before the battle of Wilson's Creek, naive national assumptions about a quick resolution with little bloodshed were dashed as armies clashed at Bull Run, Virginia. Over two-thousand five hundred men total on both sides were killed or wounded in this highly disorganized confrontation. While appalling, the numbers only hinted at future battles when many thousands would be wounded or killed. Fletcher read the battle descriptions and list of casualties, probably with great consternation. Like most pro-Union people, he likely believed the federal forces would quickly win these initial conflicts. In spite of great disappointment in the first battle, Tom quickly settled in with his unfulfilling but important job. The demands upon him increased in

August, 1861, when Martial Law was declared in St. Louis. By the end of the month, the entire state fell under martial law.[70] Events in the East resounded in the West creating great uneasiness. In preparation for the worst to come, St. Louis' Jefferson Barracks became one of the largest military hospitals in the United States with over three-thousand beds. Fletcher infrequently returned to De Soto to be with his family from then on. While family responsibilities fell on the shoulders of Tom's older brothers, they too were planning on enlisting at some point. Tom would help them when that time arrived.

In the same month, the special committee of the convention met again due to the declared state emergency. The state's elected leadership, governor, lieutenant-governor, and secretary of state, had been essentially vacated by the pro-South office holders. The convention appointed Hamilton R. Gamble as governor, William P. Hall lieutenant-governor, and Mordecai Oliver secretary of state. They were to serve until elections could be held in November. While some questioned the legality of this action, President Lincoln formally recognized the new Missouri government within a few days.[71] At the same time, John Charles Freemont, the newly appointed commander of federal forces in Missouri, began implementing his will upon the state—to the concern of Gamble and others who questioned the general's abilities. In late August, Fremont declared Martial Law in the state thus abrogating Gamble's authority over state troops and expanding the role of the military—including the role of the Provost Marshal. Fletcher served, essentially directly under Justus McKinstry, the officer who answered directly to Fremont. The Provost Marshal functioned as mayor, district attorney, and police commissioner. The department screened newspapers, censored and seized some mail; investigated rumors, assessed fines and leveed banishment orders.

One of Fletcher's particularly important duties involved preventing rebel sympathizers, who might give aid and comfort to the enemies, from leaving St. Louis County.[72] Fletcher oversaw the issuance of passes only

---

[70] Robert I. Vexler, *St. Louis: A Chronological and Documentary History*, Oceana Publications, Inc., (Dobbs Ferry, New York, 1974), 21.

[71] Parish, *History of Missouri*, 31.

[72] Primm, *Lion of the Valley*, 257.

to those who signed a *"loyalty pledge."* This simple pledge assured that the person swore allegiance to the state and federal constitution, agreed not to take up arms against the state or Union or give aid or comfort to the enemy. Fletcher supported this oath requirement. Later he referred to it as a reasonable requirement as opposed to more radical suggestions that would cause great antagonism across the state as former Southern supporters tried to adjust to the Reconstruction Period.

Using his influence, Tom did arrange for the release of two Confederate prisoners, his uncles Ben Boson Byrd and John Thomas Byrd.[73] Another more controversial duty included confiscation of property owned by Missourians who had left to join the rebel army.[74] His responsibilities, however, did not place him near battlefield action. The reports about battle engagements, mostly negative, continued to pour in to St. Louis through military and civilian channels. Tom desperately wanted to be on the front lines. His popularity in the St. Louis area led his political friends to want him to be nowhere near the front lines.

The ineptitude of General John C. Fremont, who temporarily commanded the western federal troops, and the rigidity (*and probable corruption*) of Fremont's Provost-Marshal, Justus McKinstry, may also have contributed to Fletcher's efforts to leave his post as soon as he could.[75] But the general lack of success in the East and importance of the war in the West may also have spurred him to try to change his own situation.

Finally, knowing the desperate need for more troops, in April, 1962, with permission from his superiors, he began recruiting volunteers for the 31st Missouri Volunteer Infantry. His efforts, encouraged by Frank Blair, now General Frank Blair, and reluctantly supported by his Republican political allies, were extremely successful in a short period of time.

---

[73] Zoe Booth Rutledge, *Our Jefferson County Heritage*, Ramfre Press, St. Louis, 1973, 231.

[74] Primm, *Lion of the Valley*, 258.

[75] McKinstry, called "The Terrible Provost" ruled with an iron hand and later was court-marshalled for "irregularities" in the Quartermaster Corps but exonerated. He had suggested Grant to be commander of Federal Troops in the west and remained Grant's friend throughout his life. Later he served in the U. S. Senate.

Both his brothers, John William and Charles Carroll also enlisted and eventually served under Tom.[76] He shortly obtained close to a thousand men from St. Louis and the surrounding communities: especially St. Louis, Carondelet, and Ironton. In early May, after this remarkable effort, he wrote to Irwin Z. Smith, a friend in De Soto, *"...I am off for the war, have been given a commission and have organized a regiment. You will meet me no more in the court room until the power of the Federal Government is restored in the seceded states and until, as I believe, Freedom has been secured to every creature."*[77] Fletcher knew what he fought for. And, now he would get his chance.

---

[76] Oliver R. Pechmann, *The Hero from Jefferson County: Thomas Clement Fletcher, Missouri*, 7

[77] Letter signed Thomas C. Fletcher, De Soto, MO., to Irwin Z. Smith, May 17, 1861, Missouri Historical Museum Archives, Civil War Collection, St. Louis, Missouri.

Tom Fletcher Goes to War

He officially took command as Colonel of the 31st Missouri Voluntary Infantry Regiment on October 7, 1862.[78] Samuel P. Simson, late of the 12th Missouri State Militia Cavalry, joined him as second in command. Assumption of this responsibility and opportunity had not been automatic for Fletcher. There were many St. Louisians who really wanted Fletcher to go in another direction. He had built positive relations with the leadership of the city. Many did not want him to leave Missouri. While he had successfully focused on military matters in the Provost-Marshal's office, Fletcher's recognized leadership and skill as Assistant Provost-Marshal and his local political involvement resulted in Radical Republicans courting him to run for the U. S. House of Representatives. With his reputation and contacts in the community, especially the Germans of St. Louis, he would have been an ideal candidate. He turned them down.[79] Now he wanted to fight, not work in congress. However, he would not close the door on that possibility for the future.

---

[78] Fredrick H. Dyer, A Compendium of the War of the Rebellion, V.III, c1908, 1334-1335.

[79] St. Louis Post-Dispatch (St. Louis, Missouri), August 6, 1877, 3.

His brief training began at Jefferson Barracks located along the Mississippi River in south St. Louis City. The oldest military institution west of the Mississippi, JB (*as it was and is called*) began operations in 1826. While its main function in 1862 centered on recruitment and training, in the same year the construction of the Western Sanitary Commission's hospital facilities began there. General Freemont had encouraged and protected this important establishment as soon as he took command of the western federal armies. Not a military organization, the hospital's support came from the St. Louis community. Led by Reverend William Greenleaf Eliot (one of the founders of the notable Washington University) and James E. Yeatman (later head of the United States Freedmen's Bureau and a personal friend of Tom Fletcher), its medical mission focused on assisting the wounded of both sides during the Civil War. Its humanitarian mission co-existed on the campus where Fletcher and his men studied and practiced the art of war.

Tom eagerly learned as much as he could about military command at Jefferson Barracks.[80] Lieut. Colonel Simpson and he became close friends and worked well together. Tom took everything very seriously as he knew his decisions and leadership could determine whether his men lived or died.

Fletcher and his raw troops learned at least the basics of military operations during their brief stay. Marching and completing fighting drills were part of the daily routine for the Civil War soldier. The new warriors learned how to march in columns and move into and out of formations. They learned how to follow the steps for loading, priming and firing their muskets. Hours of repetitive drills made each movement instinctual. The drill was important as infantry usually fought in two ranks (or rows) of soldiers, each man in the rank standing side by side. Tom had to bring his men to their assigned positions and fight alongside of them while making tactical decisions or responding to orders that could change in the blink of an eye. Infantry battlefield tactics had changed

---

[80] Fletcher, shortly after the end of the war, appointed Simpson Adjutant General of the State of Missouri. Simpson remained a friend of Fletcher and participated with in in many veterans' activities, especially the Grand Army of the Republic (G. A. R.) for years after.

very little since the War of 1812 or maybe even the Revolutionary War.[81] Perhaps the only significant change in training was the addition of better skirmishing tactics. They learned how to use the natural terrain to move, fire and cover themselves as needed.

Fletcher had to learn these practices as he would lead his men into battle. He took his responsibility seriously. He worked right alongside of his men; also learning. While they rested at the end of the day, he interacted with the officer corps to expand his own special requirements. His legal background and the experience of being a Provost-Marshal prepared him well for the rigidity of military life. Orders were orders and his sense of duty assured his compliance; even with foolish instructions based upon an inadequate understanding of dangerous situations. One thing Tom soon understood: his men and he had developed a bond that would last as long as they lived. In the St. Louis training, his men watched him eat the same food they ate, live in the same conditions as they did, march like they did, and learn about weapons and fighting alongside of them. They watched their Colonel Fletcher do everything he could to take care of them. Tom made sure his men had what they needed—new uniforms, weapons, food, shelter, and discipline. He would never them down.

As the training continued, Fletcher probably paid close attention to the health needs of his men. An article in the *St. Louis Republican* in May, 1861, had told the public what the soldiers needed to know about healthy living. Their instructions included:

- Never sit directly on the ground; always use a hat, scarf, blanket or something else to keep the dampness off;
- When thirsty, rinse the mouth out several times before drinking;

---

[81] This plan of battle engagement had been developed due, in part, to the fact that the muskets used were smooth-bore. Their limited accuracy demanded that the firing be performed in volleys so to "shoot in the general direction" of the enemy. This also required combatants to be close to the enemy. By the time of the Civil War, while the old muskets were in use to some degree, new rifles whose accuracy had been expanded significantly meant that the engagements would be far more devastating and be able to kill more men at much greater distances.

- Never have a heavy meal after sunset;
- Drink a cup of coffee after any major exertion;
- Do not have a big meal before a long march or going into battle;
- Take a drink of brandy after major exertions;
- Never sleep without some kind of cover; even in the summer months;
- Learn how to use a tourniquet in case a friend needs one;
- Know that a bullet to the abdomen is usually fatal; keep the person warm, give him water and help him to rest as comfortably as possible;
- Grow a three-inch beard to help warm the lungs;
- Keep hair cut to one and one-half inches and wash it and the face every day;
- Avoid fats and fatty meat in the summer months;
- Bathe regularly; being clean makes one feel better;
- Keep their nails cut and well-trimmed;
- Wear loose shoes to give toes some room;
- When using river water for drinking or cooking, boil it first; it will taste better and get rid of any impurities;
- Evacuate their bowels daily;
- Drink water mixed with corn meal each morning to assist the bowel movement process and
- Know that

  o *"to have 'been to the wars' is a life-long honor increasing in advancing years.... To have died will be the boast and the glory of your children's children.*[82]

The long hours of drilling and planning eventually paid off. Fletcher probably felt ready to go into battle after a month or so of rigorous training. Or, at least that seemed logical to him at the time.

After about seven weeks of training, his brigade was attached to Cape Girardeau, District of Missouri, First Brigade, Fourth Division,

---

[82] *Republican,* May 11, 1861, 1.

Sherman's Yazoo Expedition.[83] Orders to expeditiously move out of St. Louis stirred the brigade. Fletcher's men gathered their belongings and orderly marched down to the awaiting steamboat as soon as possible. Tom had assured that his troops had all they needed for the campaign. They carried the best weapons, wore the best clothing and had all the needed equipment available from the quartermaster corps. When the soldiers crisply stepped on the steamboat, each man knew that Col. Fletcher could be counted on to take care of them to the best of his ability. Fletcher, with pride, probably stood at the rail and watched his now well-trained (at least as well as could be expected after only a few weeks of intense effort) men orderly board and begin their great adventure. Down the Mississippi, sailing past Cairo, and then on to meet with Sherman, Fletcher's brigade rushed to join the grand campaign to control the Mississippi River. He did not have much time to worry about the future conflict. The battle would begin almost immediately upon arrival. It would take place near a Confederate embattlement located adjacent to the fortress that the city Vicksburg had become. Just a little over two months after his appointment as Colonel, Fletcher entered his first engagement— Chickasaw Bayou on December 28, 1862. It almost became his last.

At this time, the war was not going well in the east for the North; and not perfectly executed in the West either. Confederate General Price had further retreated to central Arkansas after losing the battle of Pea Ridge, Arkansas. At the time, many feared he could be moving toward Vicksburg to provide reinforcements, but no one knew for sure. Missouri had settled into chaos. Outstate Missouri burned with guerilla skirmishes and terroristic actions by undisciplined brigands sometimes calling themselves *Confederate Irregulars*. Disorderly Federal troops from Kansas maneuvered in western Missouri; sometimes indiscriminately acting little better than the guerillas. St. Louis based Federal troops ineffectively spread out thinly across the eastern side of the state as demand, and numbers permitted. Confederate raiders and guerrillas made life precarious outstate for pro-Union supporters, of which there were many. Neighbor stopped trusting neighbor and the civilian death

---

[83] Ibid.

toll slowly rose. Safety and civility quickly disintegrated and eroded into anarchy. By the end of the war much of Missouri would look like a war zone. Fletcher knew about the difficulties in the outstate regions but had his own problems as he approached his new assignment along the Mississippi River near Vicksburg.

Grant's campaign would make or break the general war in the West; but Missouri remained mostly on its own. Fletcher probably knew little of the *"grand strategy"* but had confidence in his commanders. And, he felt excited to be part of the noble effort. The most strategic point in the western campaign was the city of Vicksburg. It had to be taken in order to cut the Confederate states apart, control the Mississippi river and thus eliminate Confederate supply lines from the west. Grant placed a significant responsibility on the controversial Wm T. Sherman's shoulders. Sherman's checkered career had led to a command in the east that had not gone well. Sherman had a nervous breakdown a few months earlier and entered a period of depression that led many to consider him "crazy." Only after brilliantly supporting Grant at the battle of Shiloh did he regain the favor of federal commanders and become a friend of General Grant who had his own detractors.

Originally, Sherman's orders were to prevent Southern troops from getting between the city of Vicksburg and Grant's army and, if possible, move into Vicksburg from the rear.[84] Circumstances changed as frequently happens when conflict actually begins. Grant believed that a new strategy would be more effective. In December of 1863, Grant quickly ordered him instead to take the key point leading directly to Vicksburg: Chickasaw Bayou. This would open up a direct conduit to the city for Grant to utilize.

But, by the middle of December, Confederate cavalry had severed communication between Grant and Sherman leaving Sherman making decisions blind.[85] Fletcher's brigade operated under Frank Blair

---

[84] U. S. Grant, *Personal Memoirs, Vol. I*, Charles L. Webster & Company (New York), 1885, 430.

[85] Major Gray M. Gildner, *The Chickasaw Bayou Campaign*, unpublished thesis presented to the U.S. Army and General Staff College, Fort Leavenworth, Kansas, 1991, 2-5.

who received his orders from Sherman. Sherman attempted to flank Confederate General John C. Pemberton but ran into fortified positions occupying the high ground at Chickasaw Bayou. General Frank Blair sent Tom Fletcher, with a few trusted aides to reconnoiter the Confederate position before the battle. Leaving behind anything that might cause noise, Tom and his men worked their way carefully and stealthily across the marsh and up the hillside. The Confederate position ahead of them, Fletcher soon realized, was formidable.

The chest-deep, fifty-yard wide bayou lay directly in front of any advance and was choked by a thick entanglement of trees broken intermittently by swampland. Fletcher found Confederate-felled trees, brackish swamp, dense brush, and chest-high water in and around the bayou. Also seen were strategically placed rifle pits, and hastily built but substantial fortifications behind the rifle pits manned by riflemen and artillery.[86] The lack of standing trees provided a clear field of fire for rebel marksmen, cannons and the barricaded defenders. The Confederate editor of the Richmond Examiner later noted that the federal troops had faced a *"...whole bluff, extending a distance of two miles...frowning with guns, all of which would bear upon an enemy."*[87] After his successful but disheartening reconnoiter, Fletcher described the almost unassailable position to General Frank Blair. Blair passed the information to Brigadier General G.W. Morgan, commander of Third Division. Morgan had served gallantly in the Texas War for Independence in the Texas Rangers and then in the Mexican War. He had confidence in his new command and appeared to want to prove his value to General Sherman. Morgan discounted the information from Colonel Fletcher and assured Sherman they would be on the top of the hill in ten minutes after commencing the attack. He cited his overwhelming number of Federal troops, the enthusiasm of his men, and the lack of significant experienced opposition. Sherman listened closely and knew that he needed to control Chickasaw Bluffs in order to provide an opening that could be used to

---

[86] Ibid. 86-88; 100; note: a rifle pit is about three feet deep and four feet long with sandbags or other earth piled in front of the hole which is usually occupied by two men.
[87] Edward A. Pollard, *Southern History of the War*, C.B. Richardson, (New York), 1866, 532.

attack Vicksburg. Knowing the calculated risk, and relying on Morgan's experience, Sherman ordered the attack.[88]

Blair's forces would begin the battle. Blair decided that Fletcher's brigade would lead the left flank and be first to draw fire. Fletcher may have been skeptical at best. But, orders were orders. He assembled his officers, and then helped his men prepare. He would not let his friend, Blair down. Nor, would he abandon his troops. Whatever happened to them would also be his own fate. Christmas day, usually a day of joy, provided the time to prepare for the next day's attack. Celebrating the holiday, the best they could, the men and Fletcher likely sang songs around the campfires lighting up the sky that night and warily faced the next day. One Federal favorite of the day, *"Just Before the Battle, Mother,"* surely graced the evening repertoire. Many of the young men had no sweethearts yet; they were too young. The stanza, *"Farewell, Mother, you may never press me to your heart again; but, oh, you'll not forget me, Mother; if I'm numbered with the slain"* may have led to many sleeplessness nights among the young federal soldiers.

Under General Frank Blair's orders and according to plan, about noon on December 26th, Fletcher led his determined men in a bayonet charge through the marsh, across the dense brush, up the hill, and directly into the withering gunfire of Confederate entrenched forces.

Fletcher, immersed in the fog of battle, experienced an almost inexplicable scene of horror. Men fell beside him; his men. Some were dead; others screaming in pain. The smell of gunpowder permeated the entire front while the smoke from the rifles of each side covered the killing fields with an unreal wispy blur.[89] The noise of cannon, rifle, and men assailed the ears of all. And yet, the Union advance appeared to be making some headway at first. Fletcher, intent upon attaining the summit with his men, may or may not have worried about his brothers who were also engaged. More likely, he just moved onward toward the objective

---

[88] Thomas C. Fletcher, *Life and Reminiscences of General Wm. T. Sherman*, (Baltimore, H.V. Woodward, 1891), xiv.

[89] Smokeless bullets did not get made until the middle of the 1870's. After a few minutes of battle, especially in close proximity of the enemy would look like a fog creeping over the scene.

hoping beyond hope that a miracle would happen. While successful in taking the first and then the second set of rifle pits located in front of the main fortifications, they could go no further.[90] Everything fell apart. And, then it was over—all over.

Fellow officer, Major Milton Miles, described the futile attempt, "*The charge failed and we were so near the enemies works we could not retreat without being shot in the backs and to be shot in the back was considered amongst soldiers an evidence of cowardice, so there was nothing left for us to do except to surrender. It was a bold, fierce but fruitless engagement.*"[91] The disastrous battle resulted in Union causalities of two-hundred and eight killed, one-thousand and five wounded and five-hundred and sixty-three missing.[92] Miles shortly found out that Fletcher had become a wounded, fellow captive. The war he had so wanted to be part of ended for Fletcher, he probably thought— almost correctly. Rebel bayonets pointed at him as Tom sat on the ground with other captives seemed to be pretty definite. Hastily bandaging his minor wounds, Fletcher and fellow captives were soon ordered on their feet. They began to march. Each step he felt the pain but

The "Prison Bridge" over the Pearl River, drawn by Fletcher and published by *Harper's Gazette*; Public Domain.

likely felt determined to be an example to his men without complaining.

The Yankee prisoners were taken first to Vicksburg where the

---

[90] Gildner, *Chickasaw Bayou*, 133.

[91] Personal Papers of Major Milton Mills, 16th OVI Letter from Benjamin Heckert Description of Battle of Chickasaw Bayou December 21, 1904, *www.mkwe.com*.

[92] Gildner, Chickasaw Bayou, 147.

Confederate surgeons tended to Fletcher's wounds before incarcerating him. The unexpected number of prisoners taxed the abilities of the city to deal with them. Every available cell in city jails, cellars in buildings, and any other even remotely secure location were filled with prisoners of war (POWs). They were a serious problem. They were a burden on the city in manpower, food, and general resources. The city had been girding up for a possible siege; prisoners were a serious complication. The POW's felt their captors' annoyance and disdain. The almost rotten food did little to bolster their feelings. The constant cold and damp environments further caused illness and felt torturous. Fletcher later noted the *"barbarity of our treatment by the rebels"* both there and later in Jackson.[93] After a month of this, the rebels decided the prisoners needed to be removed from the city. Fletcher and many of the other officers along with their troops were marched to Jackson, Mississippi. Over three-hundred

prisoners were housed on an old wooden, covered bridge located over the Pearl River. Part of the bridge had already fallen into the river but the rebels had shored it up and closed the end over the water with planks. Of course, no insulation, beds, furniture, windows

The Libby Prison in Richmond, Virginia; Public Domain.

or privies were provided. Due to fear of fire, the prisoners were not allowed any heat and had to deal with cold as they could. Many did not survive.[94] Fletcher, while he had not been born to "privilege," had never

[93] "The Prison at Jackson, Mississippi," *Harper's Weekly*, New York, New York, June 6, 1863, 362-363.

[94] Ibid.

been treated like this. Even the slaves he had seen in Jefferson County lived a better life than he did in his captivity. Trying to achieve the basics of survival became almost his only focus while on the bridge. An indelible wound on his soul developed as he watched friends' dead bodies removed each morning. After a little over a month suffering under these conditions, the officers were transferred to Libby Prison at Richmond, Virginia.[95] Fletcher likely felt depressed and frustrated but also relieved to be away from the death bridge. Colonel Fletcher had spent his thirty-sixth birthday on the prison bridge in Jackson. Libby Prison would be only little better.

The three-story, forty-five thousand square foot, old tobacco warehouse sat on a hill near the James River in Richmond, Virginia. The Libby building had running water (one of the few in the area) and had been known as the Libby & Son Ship Chandlers & Grocers. Its location in a less populated part of town and accessibility by both railroad and water made it very valuable and secure for the Confederate purposes. It would be an excellent prison and, while not totally escape-proof, few successful escapes occurred during the war.

Each floor contained three large open rooms with the ground floor reserved for administration and staff. At the end of each floor were four small, barred windows. Prisoners had to stay at least three feet away from the windows. The window openings had no glass and armed guards surrounded the exterior. Inmates soon learned that putting one's head out could draw rifle fire. The cellar remained unused except for disciplinary purposes when Fletcher arrived but would be occupied by prisoners later in the war.

Fletcher found Libby worse than expected. Prisoners slept on the floor and, according to Baron Rudolph Warner, a briefly held prisoner concurrent with Fletcher's incarceration,

The treatment of the Union officers at the Libby prison is most outrageous.... most of them without even wooden boxes to sleep in, and only filthy blankets for bed clothes.

---

[95] Ibid.

The filth is most disgusting and the whole place is alive with vermin. There are nearly 250 officers confined there. The bread supplied to them is decent but the meat is decayed and stinking—much of it mule meat. Capt Turner, the Provost Marshal, who is in charge of the Libby Prison, is a perfect brute in human shape, who delights in heaping abuse upon the unfortunate victims who fall into his hands.[96]

The Confederate military did not allow furniture and provided only makeshift privies on each floor. Dysentery and diarrhea were constant companions. Malnutrition further complicated prisoners' lives. The winter cold and damp permeated the flesh of the POWs. Soldiers kept themselves occupied as best as possible. Little communication arrived from the outside and news usually arrived when additional captives entered the prison. On some rare occasions mail from home and "care packages" were allowed. The letters, however were highly censored if allowed at all. Colonel F.F. Cavada noted that the men played cards, created debating groups, gave speeches, discussed philosophy, lamented their condition, investigated *mesmerism,* carved items from broom-handles, cleaned their quarters to their best abilities, played leap-frog, participated in prayer groups and services led by chaplains, and attempted to remain civil to each other.[97]

Fletcher lived at the Richmond prison until his exchange in late April, 1863.[98] During the five-months as a POW, he spent much time in reflection. As a young man opposed to slavery, he had seen much

---

[96] *Detroit Free Press* (Detroit, Michigan), March 21, 1863, 3; *Richmond Dispatch* (Richmond, Virginia), May 8, 1863, 1; *The Fremont Weekly Journal* (Fremont, Ohio), May 8, 1863,1. Thomas Turner, eventually promoted to Major, burned as many records as possible before leaving before Federal Troops liberated the prison. After living in Canada for a time he returned to Mississippi and never had to account for his behavior as commandant of the prison.

[97] F.F. Cavada, *Experiences of a Prisoner of War in Richmond, VA, 1863-64*, King and Baird, Philadelphia, Pennsylvania, 1864, 41-58.

[98] Early in the war both sides exchanged prisoners; that practice ended after the Fort Pillow Massacre of unarmed Union African-American soldiers by troops under Nathan Bedford Forest.

depravation among the slaves. Now he personally experienced the loss of control, dignity, and sometimes even hope. Fletcher also used his artistic abilities, minimal as they were, to draw the circumstances under which he lived. Using lined paper and what ink he could scrounge; his work began to fill a small packet. One of his topics, however, dealt not with Libby Prison, but of the bridge that had scarred his psyche. This, he kept close to him in a kind of catharsis. He never wanted to forget this experience. He had survived this horror and would survive at Libby. As a senior officer, he also would have done what he could to brighten the spirits of his fellow prisoners and try to stay encouraged, hoping for a for a prisoner exchange. This experience would stay with him for the rest of his life. It may also have affected his health as, thereafter, Fletcher experienced frequent bouts of lung problems including pneumonia.

Arriving in Annapolis in early May, Maryland, Fletcher recuperated for a short time in the hospital. While there, he shared his art with some of the staff and other patients. One of the staff members believed his drawing of the Pearl River bridge deserved attention and his story needed to be told. He submitted it to *Harper's Weekly*. This well-known, New York based paper chronicled the war using illustrations and first-hand stories. Fletcher's narrative about his capture and incarceration certainly qualified for a place in the June 6, 1863 edition. His drawing of the bridge was reproduced; with some improvements for art sake. By the time of its publication, Tom felt almost recovered and looked forward to rejoining his regiment. His wife, Clara and his family surely knew of the article which probably caused them great pain knowing how he had suffered.

Lithograph of the "Battle of Chattanooga;" Public Domain.

In early August, 1863, Tom rejoined Sherman's Army of the Tennessee (River). Within a few months Colonel Fletcher's brigade moved southward with Sherman. Grant had ordered Sherman to command the Union efforts around Chattanooga, Tennessee, where the Confederates were entrenched. Their occupation and command of the high ground prevented Federal forces from moving toward Atlanta, the major supply center of the South. Sherman planned on removing immediate Southern resistance and then advance southward to further split the Confederacy. He had to first move south through Chattanooga, Tennessee, toward Atlanta. With this success, he would occupy Atlanta to deprive the remaining rebel troops from supplies and demoralize the rebel populace. Sherman, after success in Atlanta, planned to move toward Savanna, Georgia, on the coast thus completing the split. Lookout Mountain stood as the first significant obstacle.

Fletcher served under Major General John A. Logan. In mid-November, 1863, Fletcher's brigade confronted the rebels at Lookout Mountain. Later he reminisced about the "glittering bayonets" and planting "our flag on top of the mountain."[99] He and Logan continued a friendship after the war and often spoke at veterans' conventions and lobbied together for the Grand Army of the Republic.

Flanking actions, misdirection movements and direct assaults resulted in a Northern Victory in this campaign. This assured the Federal control of the Tennessee River, the rails in and around Chattanooga, and pushed the rebels southward—just as Sherman planned. The brutal assaults and fierce fighting combined with the winter weather caused logistical problems but did not result in great casualties for the Union forces in the successful campaign. Fletcher had fought alongside of his men as they trudged up the mountainside crossing boulders and fallen trees under the Confederate fire. Unlike some others who "led from the rear," Fletcher's determined efforts gave him the reputation of being a true fighting-officer. He might have remembered his friends who had fallen at Chickasaw Bluffs and earnestly committed himself to caring for his men standing right beside them as they experienced this battle. His

---

[99] *The Inter Ocean* (Chicago, Illinois), July 8, 1872, 2.

willingness to risk his own life and demonstration of gallantry probably added to the positive relationship that developed between Tom and Logan and also with Sherman.

Fierce resistance from first Confederate General Joseph E. Johnston and later by General John Bell Hood marked the remainder of Sherman's campaign. Fletcher remained active throughout the early part of the Atlanta Campaign after the success at Lookout Mountain. His brigade slowly moved toward the city of Atlanta, daily encountering the rebels. Fletcher mostly stayed in his saddle throughout the campaign getting little rest as he and his men confronted the determined rebels over and over. On May 28, the Southern troops launched a direct attack on Logan and Fletcher's positions. The Union troops held, with great effort. Only a few weeks after the initial Federal success and just before the final battles of Dallas, Georgia, Fletcher finally succumbed to the inevitable. He had become too ill to sit on his horse, suffering from battle exhaustion and perhaps pneumonia. Although resisting any effort to remove him from his men, Fletcher finally had to be relieved from duty due to his severe illness. Sherman sent him to one of the twenty-five military hospitals in Nashville where he could recuperate.[100] Reluctantly, Fletcher complied.

While having difficulty breathing and recovering from exhaustion the during his time at the hospital, the respite provided him time to think. The most recent battles and loss of men had taken a toll on his physical health but had not lessened his conviction about the importance of the war. If anything, his resolve only heightened. But, there were times in the silence of the hospital that the previous few years stood vividly in his mind and nagged at him. Free time could also cause him to look at the past with a clearer eye. He likely took stock with his life and certainly, with his military experiences. He probably thought about the major events in his life that had shaped him: his family, his upbringing, and, of course Clara and his children. He certainly ached for reunion with them but probably also wondered about it. Fletcher's experiences in the war had changed him in some subtle and some not so subtle ways. His determination to

---

[100] "Fletcher," *Ladies' Repository*, 365.

free the slaves only intensified as he saw the tremendous loss of life that had occurred with that goal in mind. But, there were other influences with which he now had to deal. He no longer just looked at himself as an abolitionist, husband, father, attorney and Missourian. He was a veteran and owed a debt to his fellow soldiers. He would never forget that. These feelings probably began on the prison bridge over the Pearl River after the Battle of Chickasaw Bluffs as he watched his fellow captives suffer, overcome adversity or die.

Tom Fletcher Back in Missouri

From the hospital in Nashville, as soon as he could travel, he journeyed home to De Soto for twenty days of leave.[101] Upon arrival, he hugged his wife and children for the first time in over two years.[102] How much rest he could get probably depended upon his family and friends in the town. They all wanted to reassure themselves that he really had recovered. Clara certainly had to limit visitors; she did so gladly.

The time at home went quickly. It did allow the weary Colonel some rest and recuperation. By the time he had to report to headquarters, he had almost regained his strength. He returned to St. Louis in December of 1863 to reassume his military duties. His illness had worried his wife, Clara. She probably worried about his return to active service in the military. His warm reception from his neighbors and friends in the St. Louis and Jefferson County certainly assisted the improvement of his health.

Political friends in St. Louis particularly had paid attention to his return. His health seemed just fine to them. In fact, he appeared to be just perfect. The Radical Republicans had already selected Tom to be their

[101] Thomas Fletcher, Letter to Colonel, June 22, 1863, Missouri Historical Society Fletcher Collection.
[102] "Life and Times," 4.

candidate for governor. The political leaders of the Republican Party were excited for the opportunity to meet with him. They wanted to get him involved with their plans for the next election. Tom should have taken notice of their lack of interest in his own ideas; he evidently didn't. Only later would he understand what they wanted from him. To be fair, he really couldn't do anything about the election activities at the time. And he really wanted to be part of the political process.

But, he still had military duties and needed to get back to his post. He reported in for duty at Jefferson Barracks in St. Louis. Command headquarters appeared wary of everything as they worried about General Price's Arkansas based army. The military and civilian populace of St. Louis feared Southern troops might possibly move toward the city. Few Federal troops remained in the entire state. St. Louis appeared ripe for takeover by a determined enemy. Fletcher's first duty upon return to active service involved the recruitment of volunteers to form the 50th and 47th Missouri Voluntary Infantry Regiments. General William Rosecrans, the Western Commander, believed Fletcher's success in recruitment at the beginning of the war made him the best qualified person for the crucial job. Fletcher immediately began the effort. His reputation had grown during the Atlanta military campaign and he had earned the respect of the citizens. They looked carefully at Fletcher and realized that he could lead and be trusted. He quickly organized the 47th unit and then became its colonel.

Meanwhile politics also engulfed him. The Radical Republicans were poised to take over the state government in the upcoming 1864 election. They believed the popularity of Lincoln would create a windfall for the Radical Republicans. But they needed a strong candidate who would appeal to voters. In this effort the German community in St. Louis would be pivotal. Fletcher's presence and reputation filled the bill. His laudatory war record resulted in his supporters calling him "*The Hero of Chickasaw Bluffs.*"[103] His recent commendable action in the Atlanta Campaign further enhanced his standing among the voters in St. Louis. He also would appeal to soldiers who would cast absentee ballots. In the

---

[103] *Republican,* October 13, 1864, 1.

first week of June,1864, the young Colonel secured the nomination for governor as the Radical Republican candidate. Strong German support in St. Louis almost assured his selection and likely election.[104] This all happened quickly—perhaps too quickly for Tom to realize what he had let himself in for.

Positive eastern war news at this time gave hope to St. Louis. Lee certainly seemed in full retreat. But anxiety over Price continued. By late winter and early Spring of 1864, the Confederacy leaned precariously on the ropes but had not fallen. Fletcher's military duties superseded his political responsibilities in the summer of 1864 as he awaited orders. He could not, even if he had wanted to, really campaign for governor. That would have to be left to others who had the time to accomplish the task for him. The Radical Republicans felt his military service would be of more importance than campaigning anyway—Fletcher defended the state of Missouri with his gun in his hand. This image of the young, handsome, charismatic leader resounded with the voters. The fact that it was true probably also worked for him. The people of the state needed something to hold on to. Fletcher provided a perfect anchor.

Missouri citizens, especially out-state people, found themselves in a desperate condition as Fletcher began working with his new command officers and staff. Over a thousand skirmishes of one type of another had been experienced in the state between June of 1861 and June of 1864. Martial law had been declared across the state but had been mostly unenforceable. Or, perhaps "under-enforceable." Confederate brigands and "guerillas" had the run of the country side. The many local sympathizers provided them with information and supplies. Federal wagon trains and patrols were ambushed and towns raided. Federals essentially were "chasing ghosts" in the outstate area near Kansas City. The situation had been so untenable In August of 1863, General Thomas Ewing, Jr. issued General Order No. 11. This required the removal of the entire population of four pro-southern counties (Jackson, Cass, Bates and Vernon) along the western border with Kansas to deny resources to the guerrillas. Even pro-Union families had to vacate their lands. Many

---

[104] *Warrenton Banner* (Warrenton, Missouri), September 6, 1870, 4.

moved to nearby towns to await the ability to return to their homes. Others left for good. Although rescinded by another general five months later, the area remained mostly vacant as Fletcher faced southward. An unintended consequence of this vacancy became the looting and burning of many empty towns, farms and fields. This left a bitterness that would not cease even with time. In this dangerous situation, the election of 1864 would take place—if rebels didn't take St. Louis and/or Jefferson City.

Further complicating the precarious nature of outstate Missouri, many of the Union troops originally posted in Missouri had been transferred east. There were less than fifteen thousand Federal troops in almost fifty posts located across the state. Every solider possible had been diverted to the East to destroy General Robert E. Lee's Army of Virginia. Fletcher knew all of this but had his own orders—these superseded his run for office. There would be no campaign by anyone in outstate Missouri anyway—it was too dangerous for the Republican candidates. Pro-Southern citizens either could not or would not likely have much impact on the outcome of the election. They could, however, continue to exercise local control and elect or re-elect southern sympathizers to offices of Sheriff, Mayor, etc.

As the election of 1864 neared, Confederates appear to have wanted to capture St. Louis and/or Jefferson City in order to assure pro-South leadership in the state for the upcoming election. Even if they were only partially successful, being able to hold part of Missouri in Southern hands would force the Federal Government to divert soldiers from Grant and Sherman to Missouri. This might help Lee and other eastern rebel forces.

Major General Sterling Price proceeded from Pocahontas, in eastern Arkansas, up through the Missouri boot heel northward with the orders to capture stores, destroy Federal property, and cripple the railroad system. He expected to recruit up to thirty-thousand Missourians for the Confederacy and live off the land.[105] As he moved northward, the guerilla activities of "Bloody Bill" Anderson and William Clark Quantrill were stepped up under orders from Jefferson Davis' military commanders in

---

[105] Cyrus A. Peterson and Joseph M. Hanson, *The Battle of Pilot Knob*, Two Trails Publishing (Independence, Missouri), 2000. 10-12.

the west. Towns were raided, rails destroyed, bridges burned and the out-state area generally terrorized.[106] This, of course, kept possible Federal reinforcements from moving to St. Louis or Pilot Knob.

The Confederate troops under Price advanced northward in three columns, consisting of twelve thousand cavalry and mounted infantry—a misleading number. In fact, only about eight thousand had rifles and many were barefoot. They did, however, have fourteen well-supported cannons.[107] The Confederate-recognized governor of Missouri, Thomas Reynolds, accompanied the troops hoping to sleep in the liberated governor's mansion.[108] When Claiborne Jackson had died of cancer in 1862, Reynolds had become "governor in exile" and recognized by Jefferson Davis. The mood of the rebels likely appeared unfoundedly optimistic to some of the more knowledgeable Southern officers.

---

[106] *Lion of the Valley*, 272.

[107] Ibid. 17.

[108] Sean McLachlan, *It Happened in Missouri*, Morris Book Publishing Co, Globe Pequot Press, (Hartford, Connecticut), 2008, 59.

The End of the War for Fletcher

In early September, 1864, General Thomas Ewing, Jr. and the entire Missouri Federal command were certain of imminent invasion by Price. Ewing dispatched Fletcher's 47th Missouri Volunteer Infantry to Fort Davidson near Pilot Knob in southeast Missouri where the St. Louis and Iron Mountain Railroad terminated. The tip of the rebel invasion would, all believed, surely arrive near there. The fort actually was more of a "field fortification." Its earthen walls could provide a fairly effective defense against a limited infantry attack but were highly vulnerable to artillery barrages or a determined assault by overwhelming numbers. The mostly untrained men of the 47th had enlisted for six months—six months they would never forget. On the 26th of September Fletcher reached the small town to join General Ewing who had just arrived himself with four companies of the Iowa 14th Infantry. While pleased to see Fletcher, together they amassed a force of a little less than one thousand mostly untrained men and some local civilians. Many of these federal defenders had never fired a gun in anger or desperation. They did, however, know that failure would threaten their homes and families in the St. Louis area. While knowing this reality did not give them confidence, it did strengthen their resolve.

Business had come almost to a standstill back in St. Louis. Most citizens just went about their business and prayed for the best. Many checked their personal weapons to be sure they would be in working order if rebels did actually attack the city. They prepared for a possible battle with only about six thousand Federal troops spread across the city's loose defenses—a disaster waiting to happen. Everything depended upon Ewing and Fletcher stopping Price before he reached St. Louis or delaying him until federal reinforcements arrived. All eyes looked toward Pilot Knob and St. Louis citizens held their breath. Both Ewing and Fletcher were keenly aware of the precarious position they held and the importance of their stand. The two commanders, and perhaps many of the others stationed at the earthen fort, might have been thinking about the men at the Alamo back in 1836. The situation did have many similarities.

Fortunately for St. Louis, Price chose not to go straight to the city. He decided to gather the needed military stores to be found at the sparsely defended Fort Davidson located at Pilot Knob—a fateful mistake. About the same time Price turned toward Pilot Knob, federal reinforcements arrived in St. Louis effectively thwarting Price should he actually make it that far north. Neither Price or Ewing and Fletcher knew of this. The two Union commanders only hoped the Federal troops would at least arrive there in time should they fail to stop or delay the rebels. Farther west, federal troops from Kansas were moving toward Jefferson City and Rolla should Price turn in that direction—a fortuitous move by the Federal forces. Ewing and Fletcher knew that this had been planned but did not know if it was in progress. In western Missouri anything could happen; and most of it not good.

In the fortified earthen redoubts of Fort Davidson, Fletcher commanded the infantry defenders. He paced around the redoubt, his hands ready to draw both or either his sword and pistol. Like his men, but carrying the burden of command, he also watched the hills and waited for the inevitable assault. After a quick mid-day meal on September 23, 1964, the nervous Federal soldiers stood at their posts and stared at the hills beyond. The young, untested defenders probably were reassured by Fletcher who had been in many engagements. After all, he stood right alongside of them and appeared confident, calm and determined; regardless of what he really might have felt inside. Fletcher knew their situation to be questionable at best. Duty, responsibility and determination required him to be there. He would not let his men down; he never had before. Movement along the hillsides alerted the defenders of impending action. They had not long to wait. Fletcher readied his men.

About two o'clock in the afternoon, Confederate soldiers raced downs the hillside and charged the southeastern and eastern sides of the fortifications. Fletcher brought defenders from the other sides to assist in repelling the attackers. Rebel troops charged, reached the Federal redoubt and fought hand to hand. They had to pause as Union fire rained on them. In the chaos of the battle Fletcher was hit by a hand-spike but sustained no serious injury that would disable him. The rebels finally retreated having accumulated over fifteen hundred casualties. The Federal forces

Author's photo of wall art: "The Battle of Pilot Knob;" permission Wilson's Creek National Battlefield.

holding the fort temporarily rested; waiting for another assault. Some just sank to the ground where they were, and put their heads in their hands thanking God they were still alive. Fletcher later related that *"The firing ceased; not a shot was heard; the silence was broken only by the groans of the wounded who lay everywhere on the field. The enemy was scattered in the gullies, ravines, and behind logs—in every lace of concealment—waiting the coming of darkness to cover their retreat."*[109] Each man caught his breath and drank a little water to quench his dry mouth. Relief swept across the battlements. Fletcher knew that the end of the engagement had not

---

[109] *Battle of Pilot Knob,* 175.

arrived; this had been just the beginning. He moved to Ewing's side to mutually assess the next steps.

Ewing called all of his officers together to assess their situation. After a brief discussion, they all realized they could not stand another charge if accompanied by a serious cannon barrage or if hit on all sides at once by overwhelming numbers. Confederates likely did not want to lay down a heavy cannon fire as the military stores they so badly needed might be blown up. This meant that a sustained and coordinated overwhelming assault would likely be attempted. Facing this would be the remainder of Fletcher's infantry and the remaining other Federal troops and a few civilians. They had already lost over fifteen percent of their own forces, killed, wounded, or missing in this first engagement. One more attack would surely overrun them. Luckily for Fletcher and Ewing, Price decided to wait until the next day to finish the defenders.

The Union Officers discussed alternatives. There were essentially two: surrender or try to escape. Fighting to the death like the defenders of the Alamo would serve no purpose and did not come under any serious consideration. Fletcher had already been a prisoner of war and knew what they would face if they surrendered. He opposed that possible decision. After the Confederate massacre of over three hundred unarmed black soldiers at Fort Pillow, Tennessee, in April, 1864, the United States Army had refused any further exchange of prisoners. The horrors awaiting at the Southern prison camp at Andersonville were well known and only talked about in hushed tones. The officers surely knew what would likely happen to the several dozen black civilian workers who were helping them. The rebels would show no mercy and murder them all. So, surrender appeared to be out of the question.

Knowing that they could not hold out against the expected well-coordinated attack, they developed a daring plan. They would move through a perceived gap the rebel lines in the middle of the night rather than surrender. A relatively large fissure existed between rebel encampments so it did not appear impossible. That is, if everything fell into place—a big "*if.*" They had to move quietly in hopes they would not be detected. This became their plan. They began its implementation immediately after the officers' meeting. Each officer received his orders and proceeded accordingly. Fletcher would retain command of the infantry and assist in rear-guard actions as needed—protecting the main column during the tactical withdrawal. A special team began amassing gunpowder and placing it carefully to do the most damage to stores they could not take with them. Strategically located campfires were maintained and left burning to give a casual Confederate observer the idea that everything remained normal inside the fort.

Several hours before daylight they all started the escape. Soldiers and civilian aides carried all they could, ammunition, guns, and essential military supplies. All items were muffled as possible. Wounded soldiers were carried as needed or assisted by comrades; some gagged to prevent noise. Of course, a lot of valuable material remained and could not be left for the rebels. Heavy guns were spiked and all ammunition, rifles, and other military supplies were placed in the center of the redoubt. Black powder was stacked throughout the pile and alongside. Timed fuses were placed. After these preparations were made, and all personal noisy items secured, each soldier began walking in the dark, gun in hand. After the main body had been successful in their stealthy retreat and were as far away as reasonably possible before first light, the special unit lit the fuses. They then hightailed it away to rejoin the main column. Fletcher's rear guard took a defensive stand and stood ready to come to the aid of the special detail if needed as the rest of the column moved on. They did not have to; the plan worked. The special unit quickly and quietly passed through Fletcher's men and rejoined the main column.

The retreating Federal troops held their breath and kept silently marching toward Rolla. They figured they would have only a few hours head-start before the rebels figured out what they were doing. It would have to be enough. After the special unit had safely passed, Fletcher and his men soon caught up with the main column and assumed their protective positions on the rear and on each flank.

Early in the morning, just before dawn, multiple loud explosions were heard by Confederate General Price and his men. They thought an accident had occurred within the fort and the remaining Union troops would have to surrender when light broke.[110] They probably smiled at the perceived misfortune of the Yankees. At first light, a small reconnaissance group moved slowly and deliberately toward the redoubt. Upon reaching the ruins, they immediately realized what had happened—they had been outsmarted. There would be no guns, no ammunition, no field-pieces, no medical supplies, no food—no nothing. Their entire plan had fallen apart and capturing St. Louis became a futile dream. The only thing left to do would be to move toward Jefferson City. But they would first follow Ewing and Fletcher toward Rolla after the army had regrouped.

Price then sent a smaller and more mobile force to pursue the retreating Yankee troops—another mistake. The fruitless pursuit eventually cost them three more days and led them toward their own destruction. Price also sent skirmishers out in several directions to see possible Federal resistance should they need to turn northward for supplies. One small group reached as far as De Soto, where the Fletcher family lived. The rebels burned a nearby railroad bridge but did little other damage. They fired a few shots at some farmers but essentially just rode around the countryside a bit before returning to join Price.

Colonel Thomas C. Fletcher just after the "Battle of Pilot Knob;" Public Domain.

Meanwhile, Ewing and Fletcher's ragged Union troops marched orderly and quickly northwest toward Rolla and Jefferson City. They did not need silence anymore and conversations began as the men marched onward. Only a few horses remained available; Fletcher and Ewing had two of them. Dr. Sam B. Rowe, Quartermaster Sergeant, had been slightly wounded and limped along until Fletcher noticed him. Rowe related that, "... *seeing me limping along outside the ranks and sympathizing with me, he [Col. Fletcher] very kindly tendered me the use of his Bucephalus, with I rode nearly to Webster.*"[111] The *St. Louis Post-*

---

[110] Ibid., 184.
[111] Ibid., 235.

Dispatch, in 1877, described Fletcher's relationship with his troops, "...*he was kind hearted and sympathetic with his men, but a stern disciplinarian. He was, at all times, willing to endure any hardships asked of his soldiers and his good judgment and liberal and humane disposition made him almost revered by all under him.*"[112] His calm demeanor reassured his troops as they evaded the Confederate pursuers. His frequent rear-guard actions against the pursuing rebels held the enemy at bay.

The survivors reached Hermann on the 30th of September and then Rolla on the next day where reinforcements awaited. They had traveled almost seventy miles in less than forty hours of forced march. Fletcher's rear guard had been almost continually harassed by Price's advance elements. The pursuing rebels could not get near the main column because of Fletcher's guard. The Confederate forces were finally forced to discontinue their chase as the Union troops reached the safety of Rolla and the welcome arms of the reinforcements. Fletcher had made it to safety.

On October 6th, Major General Rosecrans replied to the heroic efforts against Price with General Orders, No. 189, congratulating Ewing, Fletcher and other officers noting that "*Under such commanders, Federal troops should always march to victory.*" President Lincoln later breveted Fletcher brigadier-general for his actions during and after the battle.[113]

After this setback, Sterling Price continued to move westward through central Missouri until Federal troops forced his army out of the state in late October. The rebel guerillas, however, continued making the area around Jefferson City, Rolla, and further west a very dangerous place to live, work or travel through. Elections were interrupted in many places but still held. "Governor" Reynolds never slept in the governor's mansion.

---

[112] *St. Louis Post-Dispatch* (St. Louis, Missouri), August 6, 1877, 3.
[113] Missouri State Archives, Finding Aid 3.18.

Fletcher Elected Governor

Fletcher soon returned to St. Louis to meet with the military command. After debriefing, he then made his way home to De Soto for a few days rest and recuperation. His family and friends gave him a hero's welcome. The time at home, though short, probably invigorated him. He and Clara probably began planning their likely move to Jefferson City. He felt confident that they would be moving. He also had to begin his personal participation in the gubernatorial campaign. The November election loomed near and he began campaigning as he could. Fletcher proved to be a perfect candidate for the Radical Republicans. On October 13, 1864, he traveled the short distance from De Soto to St. Louis on the Iron Mountain Railroad to make his first speech in his campaign for governor.

Missouri U. S. House of Representatives member, Henry Taylor Blow, introduced Fletcher after the candidate arrived to address the assembled crowd. Blow, formerly the U.S. Ambassador to Venezuela appointed by Abraham Lincoln, had supported abolition all his life. His father had freed Dred Scott after the Supreme Court declared Scott no more important than a table or a cow. Scott's "owner" had given him to Blow for a nominal (and therefore legal) sum. Blow and Fletcher had been friends since before the war and had worked together against slavery. Both had served as delegates to the exciting and momentous Chicago

Republican Convention that had nominated Lincoln. Blow had wealth and great standing in the St. Louis community.

Blow introduced Fletcher as *"The Hero of Chickasaw Bluffs"* and noted that Tom now received the laurels for his actions at Pilot Knob

> *In behalf of the loyal people of this city, it is my privilege to welcome to our confidence, our hospitality, and our enduring respect and gratitude. We have watched with intense interest the course you have pursued since your nomination for the high office of Governor of this state; and with more eager gaze and prayerful hearts have followed you in your labors for the public good, until you confronted the traitor hosts that were desolating and robbing the State which has cherished and honored them....*
>
> *I can see you now, with your brave commanders urging your men to death or victory....*
>
> *...my gallant friend, born upon the soil you have so earnestly labored to make free, and in sight of the landmark you so nobly defended, leading those fearless men who so rapidly rallied to your banner in the hour of peril and trial—how shall we reward you?*
>
> *...all is bright now, and with the welcome we give, receive also the assurances that a victorious army of voters will confer on you the 1ˢᵗ Radical Governor of Missouri....*
>
> *His triumph will toll the death knell of slavery and make Missouri free.... Let us stand united, and that glorious day will soon dawn upon us.*[114]

Blow set the stage and tenor of the campaign. Fletcher, the military hero, will lead Missouri into a state of freedom for all people—ending slavery. His standing with the soldiers of the state would certainly be supportive due to Tom being *"one of them."* The Radical Republicans would likewise give him their votes and financial assistance. Those

---

[114] *Republican,* October 13, 1864, 1.

who still supported slavery were unlikely to vote in such large numbers to seriously affect the outcome. Confederate troops from Missouri, of course, were excluded from the election. Price's presence as an invading force might actually expand the Republican vote. Fear motivates votes.

Fletcher understood the very real likelihood of being elected and maintained a confident demeaner. He primarily needed to continue his current military duties, emphasize his military background, and let his excellent reputation as an honorable, capable and trustworthy man work. Even those military men who would support General George McClellan's candidacy for president against Lincoln would see Fletcher as a reasonable choice for governor. Unlike his opponent, General Thomas Price (*no relation to Confederate General Sterling Price*), Fletcher had stood in battle shoulder to shoulder with his men enduring whatever hardships they encountered. He began his campaign in a humble manner, "...*I would not on this occasion attempt to say more to you than I sincerely and heartily, from my own heart, thank you for the manifestation for the appreciation of the conduct of the men whom I had the honor to command at Pilot Knob.*"[115]

Fletcher went on to give credit to General Ewing and the men serving under him.

> ...*If there was good fighting there, and on the march to Leesburg, and at Leesburg it was done by the soldiers. The little I did there, in so far as my limited ability in that line enabled me to do, was to show those men who had not been drilled a sufficient length of time to make as thoroughly soldiers as they were capable and to show them how the fighting ought be done....*[116]

Fletcher continued through this first speech to give credit to Ewing, Major [David] Murphy, Captain Frank Dinger (who had been killed fighting a rear-guard battle with Fletcher against the pursuing rebels), Lieutenant Tuttle (who happened to be in the audience), Colonel Maupin, Captain Leper, Captain McMurty, Major Williams, and Lieutenant

---

[115] Ibid.

[116] Ibid.

Colman. Fletcher went into some detail about the battle and the forced-march thereafter for the enthralled crowd. He derided the Confederate "Governor" of Missouri and, to the delight of the audience, suggested the Southerner likely would not get many votes in the upcoming election. He thanked the audience for the response to his fellow military men and promised they would continue the fight until "Old Pap" Price had been defeated. Then he briefly turned to the State itself

> *I would like to talk of the vast wealth to be derived in time to come from the culture of the rich and fertile prairies of the State that stretch themselves away toward sundown. I would like to talk to you about the vast wealth that is to be derived, particularly in your great commercial city here, from the vast manufacture of all the vast industrial resources which are spread out toward the southwest, where the interminable forests of tall pines lift their plumed hearts towards heaven, and inexhaustible mines of lead and copper lie concealed. I say it would be a pleasure to me to talk to you about tall this, and how I would, if it were in my power, lend a helping hand to the capital which is coming time is to develop these resources, tear down these mountains of iron, cut down these forests of pine, roll cut his iron for purposes which will advance civilization and contribute to the progress of our republic and all the world…but it would be impossible to do so at this time…*[117]

Fletcher explained that he would not be able to travel to places where his opponent, Thomas Lawson Price, would like to debate him as Fletcher still had military obligations. He further assured his constituents that he had never voted Democratic unless it had been a *"Benton (Thomas Hart Benton) Democrat."* While not directly condemning McClellan, neither did he support the general. He left after thanking the people for their support for the military. He did not ask them for their vote. He did not

---

[117] Ibid.

need to.[118] The 47th had mainly been recruited from the St. Louis area. Their family members and friends were well aware that they were not reading about their friends and loved ones in the obituaries or having to find out to which Confederate prison camp their family member had been taken. This, they attributed partially and, in fact, significantly to Thomas C. Fletcher. Extended families and most St. Louisians also felt warmly toward the Colonel.

He did have continuing military responsibilities. But his superiors did not press him into more active service in the effort to defeat Price during the remaining three weeks or so until the election. As the election neared, Price finally led his outnumbered and defeated troops southward—probably toward Texas. At least that would have been what most people in St. Louis thought. Federal troops followed, pushing him out of Missouri. Fletcher remained in St. Louis interacting with the command structure in whatever ways he could be helpful. This allowed him some freedom to campaign. Other Radical Republicans continued to provide most of the political outreach efforts.

The German community especially worked hard for Tom. But the entire electorate appeared more concerned with the national contest. The opposition challenged Fletcher to take a public stand regarding the national ticket and chastised him for not doing so. McClellan's opposition to Lincoln resonated somewhat in Missouri but far less so than many expected. General Price, Fletcher's opponent, strongly supported McClellan but Fletcher publicly asked for support for himself while encouraging the electorate to make their own decisions on the national ticket. If pressed, he merely stated his own support for Lincoln. In fact, Fletcher felt very confident that Abraham Lincoln would win and the president did not need his support in order to do so.

The national Republican leadership understood the importance of this election and Lincoln privately feared being defeated by McClellan. Lincoln's private secretary, John Nicolay, contacted people who would know about various areas presidential support—Missouri being one of the most questionable. Fletcher assured the president that Missouri

---

[118] Ibid.

would be on his side of the election; of that he had no worries. The Missouri military vote, which could have gone for General McClellan, supported Fletcher, who supported Lincoln. Nationally, the military supported Lincoln in the election. Absentee votes were overwhelmingly pro-Lincoln. The state of Missouri submitted its eleven electoral votes for Lincoln by a margin of a little over sixty-nine percent to a little less than thirty percent. In fact, Fletcher received almost a thousand votes more than Lincoln did. The Radical ticket did well everywhere in Missouri. It won three-fourths of the upcoming constitutional convention delegates. Further, Radical Republican Mayor James S. Thomas easily returned to office.

After the election, the convention president, Arnold Krekel and vice-president Charles Daniel Drake quickly proceeded to make plans for the upcoming convention.[119] Fletcher did not participate to any extent; his colleagues did not need or want his input in this early stage of preparation. This might have surprised the governor-elect and may have confused him too. Fletcher stood ready to lead the party but, most of all, he wanted to help the state recover from the war.

On November 18th, Thomas C. Fletcher resigned his commission because of his election as governor of Missouri. His heroic military record and moderate demeanor had contrasted well with professional politician Thomas L. Price on the Democrat side. The Radical Republican strategy had worked well.[120]

After the election, he and his family began their preparation for his assuming the governorship on January 2, 1865. He might have still believed that his position would carry enough influence to allow him to guide the reconstruction period. His political experience had been in organizing

Clara Fletcher about the time of her becoming First Lady of Missouri; permission Fletcher House Foundation.

---

[119] *Lion of the Valley*, 274.

[120] Price was not related to Southern General Sterling Price, but the name might have caused many voters to stop and think a bit....

and campaigning—not in governing. He would soon gain a strong dose of reality. Clara, probably having no misgivings about the new role for her husband, began gathering up belongings for the move to Jefferson City. The city still resembled a fort rather than a state capital. Over a thousand soldiers manned the fortifications immediately surrounding the city. Armed riverboats patrolled the Missouri and the general military presence permeated the town. Bureaucrats, soldiers, merchants, lobbyists, office holders, and politicians occupied every room of every building. The entire area seemed to be draped in black crape as instability seemed the norm in all phases of the city's business. Smiles were seldom seen among the populace. To this dismal culture came the Fletchers.

Clara probably looked forward to being First Lady. Certainly, her husband no longer would be a target for Southern soldiers. He also would be with her and her children. For her, the war had ended. For Fletcher, another conflict loomed before him as he began to look at the condition of the state. He felt confident about his ability to deal with the challenges ahead. It is likely that Tom felt that his whole life had led him to this time and place. He could look back at his election and service as Jefferson County Clerk, his role as the St. Louis Assistant Provost Marshal, his successful legal efforts for the railroads and his noteworthy military career with pride. He had learned much in each role. Now, he led the state and could restore safety and prosperity, or so he thought.

While he awaited inauguration, Fletcher did what he could to be as prepared as possible when he would begin his office. He knew that safety of the citizens of Missouri would head the list of things to address. He began to look carefully at the precarious military situation across the state. While the controversial military commander, General William Rosecrans, had some limited success in Missouri, stability and safety did not exist except in St. Louis and a few other areas mostly in eastern Missouri. Fletcher wanted to go in a different direction from Rosecrans. He obtained the removal of the general and secured his own choice, General Grenville M. Dodge.[121] Dodge had directed the Federal Intelligence network for a short time and had served with Fletcher

---

[121] *Chicago Tribune* (Chicago, Illinois), December 11, 1864, 2.

under Sherman during the Atlanta Campaign. Dodge enthusiastically joined him but couldn't stay long. Dodge also understood railroads so about a month later, when President Lincoln asked him to find a place to start the Trans-Continental Railroad, he would leave Fletcher's service. Fletcher quickly learned that at least initially, he had to rely on the Federal government for military leadership in the state. The new governor would have to learn how to deal with the transitory nature of the leadership in the Missouri-based Federal forces. The continuing demands elsewhere in the nation by the Federal army resulted in many transfers of personnel—often taken from the western commands. Keeping up with this did not prove to be an easy task for the new governor. It seemed as if just when he began to work well with one military commander the officer would be sent somewhere else and Fletcher had to start all building a relationship with the replacement all over again.

Fletcher also connected more directly with the Republican state legislative leadership. He needed to know what they were doing and obtain a better picture of his upcoming role and responsibilities. The initial meetings did not proceed as he hoped. The lukewarm response did little to make him feel a real part of the proceedings. His absence in the war had not ingratiated him with the power brokers nor made him an "insider." The Radical Republicans had "moved on" from the days of Blair and Brown. While polite, Charles Daniel Drake and the other leaders made it clear that Fletcher's input carried little weight either in the legislature or would it in the upcoming convention where the real future direction of the state would be set. They galloped ahead using their own agenda, paying little attention to the governor-elect. The party leadership quickly convened the constitutional convention in order to punish the traitors. Drake, although vice-president of the convention, actually led the Radical Union Republican Party opposing the Conservative wing. By the election of 1864, the Conservatives essentially had migrated into the Democratic Party but with reduced influence.[122] This left the Radical

---

[122] William E. Parish, *Missouri Under Radical Rule, 1865-1870*, (University of Missouri Press, Columbia, Missouri, 1965), 9-11.

Republicans in control, led functionally by Drake but publicly headed by Governor Fletcher.

Essentially, the legislature mostly expected the governor to be a figurehead. After all, he had been in the military and did not have much influence in the legislature. His youth and lack of experience did not help him either. Fletcher, however, had other ideas. He just had to figure out what he could and could not do as governor. While he certainly knew the limitations of his authority, he did have a "bully-pulpit" and could use his position to leverage positive results in other ways. He did not believe in indiscriminate punishment of those who were unruly, but he insisted on safety, stability and the potential for state growth. The new governor spent much time and thought in preparation for his first speech to the people of Missouri. Clara likely provided an attentive sounding board for her husband as he prepared his remarks. Tom needed to set the tone for his administration and demonstrate bold leadership. In Fletcher's January 2, 1865 inaugural address, he explained his own perspective for recovery:

> In the name of Truth, of Justice, of Freedom, and of Progress, God has permitted us a political triumph, bringing with it the solemn responsibility of promoting those great principles by an enforcement of the fundamental law for securing the peace, happiness and prosperity of the people of the State....
>
> Being victorious everywhere, let magnanimity now distinguish our actions, and having nothing more to ask for party, let us, forgetful of our past differences seek only to promote the general good of the people of the whole commonwealth.

He further encouraged the restoration of the state's economic and social structures. He specifically, asked for support for the families of fallen soldiers along with developing a robust educational system for the state. He wanted the general public to have the advantage a good education could provide them. A well-educated populace provided the foundation for democracy, he believed. Additional concerns were for election security, the need for an adequate militia due to the continuing state-wide violence, and a vigorous immigration effort in Europe to bring more settlers to the state. Perhaps the most controversial section centered on the need for railroads to be supported and temporarily taken over by the state.[123] The new governor had positive experiences with the railroads and knew the importance of a strong infrastructure for economic reconstruction and expansion. Fletcher's perspective toward recovery and public safety essentially mirrored that of Abraham Lincoln. Fletcher's address, while carried in its entirety by most Missouri newspapers and a few elsewhere, had little impact on those who held the power in Missouri. It found no editorial support. Likely, the population felt good about what he said but paid little real attention. Guerillas still wreaked havoc across the state. Most people paid close attention to the sections in his speech that dealt with peace and prosperity. The reaction of the African-Americans of Missouri might be summed up in a letter to the *Missouri State Times* from a soldier in the first colored regiment raised in Missouri then stationed in Helena, Arkansas, *"We had a great day yesterday. All the colored soldiers were out in full uniform, rejoicing over the friends of their friends at home...All are Fletcher men after reading his inaugural."*[124]

Meanwhile the legislature continued working on the Emancipation issue and preparing a totally new constitution. Fletcher liked their work on emancipation and probably encouraged their deliberations. But rather than amending the current Missouri constitution, Drake had decided to change the ground rules. His antipathy toward the ability of the legislature to make any lasting impact on the future of the state led him to maneuver the delegates toward his point of view. Thus, he had his own personally-developed draft new constitution ready to introduce to the group. The assembled delegates followed his lead. The St. Louis German community particularly took offence to Drake and his heavy-handiness but did not have enough power to do much about it. Their ally, the new

---

[123] Nathan H. Parker, *Handbook: The State of Missouri,* Governor's Inaugural, (P. M. Pinckard: St. Louis, 1865), 30-41.

[124] *Missouri State Times* (Jefferson City, Missouri), January 28, 1865, 2.

governor, did not even attend the convention. He had not been invited to do so.

Fletcher obviously had little impact on the proceedings although he enthusiastically supported emancipation. Parts of the proposed constitution floating around, however, worried him. Tom understood that Drake's major concern appeared to be his desire to punish the "rebels" by disenfranchising them. Drake and significant numbers of legislators also opposed giving the freed slaves the right to vote.[125] These two actions contrasted directly with the views of the new governor. There would be other problems as the convention continued its deliberations. Tom watched the legislators helplessly and with great frustration.

Regardless of these problems, as the new governor began his term, his wife, Clara, settled in as first lady. She began her efforts to create a comfortable home in the disappointing governor's "mansion." It really wasn't much of a mansion. The Fletchers were the first occupants to live in the building since before the Civil War had begun. Hamilton Gamble, the provisional governor appointed in 1861 who died in 1864 and his successor, William Prebble Hall both maintained residences in St. Louis instead of Jefferson City during the Civil War. The structure badly needed renovation but really needed to be razed and replaced with a new one. At its zenith, the mansion had been described as a *"low storied building with many wings and embowered in trees and furnished with than richness of velvet carpets, venetian mirrors and lace and brocade curtains hanging from lambrequins and held back by heavy cords…wide fireplaces and…superb antiques."*[126] That day had long since past when Clara, her husband and two children moved in. This forty-eight by thirty-foot building needed a lot of repair, but she did the best she could to make it habitable.[127]

In the time she served as the state's First Lady, she kept expenses to the minimum. The state, in dire financial difficulty, did not have the

---

[125] Drake would later support this enfranchising in order to expand the Republican electorate.

[126] Jerena East Giffen, *First Ladies of Missouri*, Wadsworth Publishing Co.; Giffin Enterprises, (Jefferson City, Missouri, 1996), 87.

[127] Ibid., 89.

money to really support the governor's living requirements—which were complicated. Tom knew that he needed to develop a positive relationship with the legislators and others with influence in the state. The simple fact was that he did not know them and they did not know him. Fletcher decided that he would meet with each of them so they could get to know each other. Of course, he could meet in their offices or in his but that would be mostly formal. He needed to create a personal relationship between him and each legislator—Republican or Democrat. He also knew that Clara and he could meet with people in a comfortable and informal manner at the mansion. Here, he could build trust, friendship and confidence with his visitors. This meant formal and informal dinners, luncheons, and teas for the wives. Clara skills as hostess and bright conversationalist would be of immense value in all of these. However, hosting such events would be expensive. With success in this tact, Tom could be effective and establish real leadership. In some ways, it was a "high risk—high reward" gamble. Above all else, he needed to be seen as a governor who would serve and lead at the same time. Whatever it took, Tom would make sure that by the end of his term, life in Missouri would be better for all citizens. The Fletchers had to personally supplement the meager resources allocated by the state legislature. The first social event, a reception, drew broad praise for the governor and his "estimable lady."[128] The youngest member of the Fletchers, Ella, appeared to revel in her position as "first daughter."[129] Throughout the term of office Clara provided stability for her children and a comfortable refuge for her husband. The two apparently had a mutually respectful and loving relationship. He needed her support as he took the reins of government firmly in hand; or tried to. She also made the old ramshackle mansion a pleasant location for many social events; even allowing wine although she did not partake nor did she personally serve it.[130] The two teen-aged Fletcher children learned deportment and participated in the normal studies for pre-teens of the day. But governmental funding did not prove adequate for the family's needs or responsibilities as the term progressed.

---

[128] Ibid.
[129] Ibid., 91.
[130] Ibid.

In the entirety of the governor's four years in office only $4,066 (about twenty-five thousand dollars a year in 2018 dollars) came from the State to support life in the "*mansion.*"[131] Entertainment and even most of the day-to-day ordinary expenditures came from the Fletchers' personal accounts.

By 1871 construction of a new mansion had begun; but that did not help the Fletchers. Under the watchful eye of the First Lady, they made do with what they had. The new governor had little time for relaxation anyway.

On January 6th, Immediately after the inauguration, the constitutional convention, led by Charles Drake, finally convened. It remained in session until April 10th. In addition to greater emphasis on education, bank and corporate encouragements, the new constitution outlined a comprehensive plan for the post-war era—essentially Drake's design.

The first issue in the legislature which passed generated little opposition: the emancipation of slaves.

> *It having pleased Divine Providence to inspire to righteous action the sovereign people of Missouri, who, through their delegates in Convention assembled, with proper legal authority and solemnity, have the day ordained:*
>
> *That hereafter, in this state, there shall be neither slavery or involuntary servitude, except in punishment of crime, whereof the part shall be duly convicted; and all persons held to service or labor as slaves are hereby declared free.*
>
> *Now, therefore, by authority of the Supreme Executive power vested in me by the Constitution of Missouri, I, Thomas C. Fletcher, Governor of the State of Missouri, do proclaim that henceforth and forever no person within the jurisdiction of this State shall be subject to any abridgement of liberty, except as the law shall prescribe for the common good, or know any master but God.*[132]

---

[131] *Holt Sentinel* (Oregon, Missouri), October 30, 1896, 9.

[132] Fletcher, Thomas C., "Proclamation of Freedom," *Missouri's Jubilee,* Jefferson City, Missouri. W.A Curry, Public Printer. 1865.

Thomas Fletcher about the time he served as Governor of Missouri; Public Domain

Former slave owners, at least those who had taken up arms against the American Flag, received no compensation.[133]

Governor Fletcher enthusiastically signed the Proclamation on January 11, 1865. Missouri became the first former slave state to free slaves. Also, in fact, Missouri became the first state to officially renounce slavery. Fletcher felt great pride in this fact and eagerly addressed the legislature. Understanding the momentous nature of this event and the public relations of it, he arranged for ten thousand copies of his "Jubilee Speech" to be printed for distribution within the state and across the nation:

Free Men of Missouri:

I thank you for the invitation you have given me to mingle my voice with yours on this occasion of our general rejoicing.... Missouri is free! ...words fail to give an impression of the real feelings of the victory.

...There is something in the feelings of an old "White Republican," an old Abolitionist, who has endured the proscriptive and intolerant rule of the arrogant slave power in Missouri for the last fifteen years, that language is entirely inadequate to express. In this free atmosphere he feels himself a head taller.

The white men of Missouri are today emancipated from a system which as so long lain with crushing weight upon

---

[133] Meyer, *Heritage,* 406-407.

their energies. We are now rid of every weight, and ready for the race. And the white man, too, is free. The gates of a bright future are open to him as well as to us.

Let us now set to work as becomes men, to rid ourselves of all the effects the damnable system of slavery has left behind it. Not the least among us are the bushwhackers, red-handed marauders and robbers, fit allies of the institution which enslaved the souls and bodies of men.

...I apprehend that we will have an efficient Militia. Those who cannot be trusted with guns will still be militia, and will not think it hard if, instead of being required to shoot their friends, the rebels, they should be detailed to the pioneer corps, the engineer corps, or the sappers and miners and be armed with axes or spades.... Roads and bridges are to be made....

There are counties in this State where the large majority of the people make no effort to enforce the laws, or to render secure the lives and property of their loyal neighbors. It may be necessary to have military force in such counties, and if so, the circumstances justifying it, that county will have to pay for the troops stationed there....[134]

In regard to the freed slaves, most in the St. Louis area had already left their *"masters."* During the war a large number of ex-slaves began migrating across the Mississippi to east St. Louis or moved into the northern segments of St. Louis city. The governor's proclamation made this all legal. It's publication by the more conservative newspaper, *The Republican,* met with little enthusiasm. They printed it below the Secretary of State, Francis Rodman's, encouragement of counties to develop well-paid local militias which he suggested would be needed in the upcoming time after the end of the war. The paper did not comment at all on the proclamation. It did, however, editorialize that it might be

---

[134] *Missouri's Jubilee; Speech of Thomas C. Fletcher,* (W.A Curry, Public Printer: Jefferson City), 1865, 4-6.

time for women over twenty-one to have the right to vote; not to hold office, but at least to vote.[135] Other state papers carried the governor's pronouncement but added little editorial comment. Nationally, however, it appeared to gain a lot of attention in the news media and in the halls of congress. People across the nation began to hear about Thomas C. Fletcher. It would not be the last time.

---

[135] *St. Louis Dispatch* (St. Louis, Missouri), January 23, 1865.

Fletcher vs Draconian Laws

As unpopular or popular as the Emancipation Proclamation might have seemed, two additional legislative orders actually enmeshed incredible bitterness across the state. The *"Ousting Ordinance"* removed the Missouri Supreme Court, all state judges, circuit attorneys, sheriffs and county recorders effective May 1, 1865. It mandated the governor to appoint over eight hundred replacements. Fletcher found himself in the middle of a maelstrom not of his own making. Understanding his responsibility and the need for some stability, he delayed some appointments and did not replace those officials deemed "loyal" and competent. Finding a large number of qualified persons would not prove easy. Fletcher left many of the decisions up to his staff and regional Radical Republican representatives; at least for the initial vetting. He did not shirk from appointing people he knew, admired and respected to positions. From across the state, opposition to this effort became vocal; very vocal. The question appeared to be, *"Would Fletcher really replace all these positions?"* He would.

Even the reviled Ousting Ordinance, a *Draconian* order, failed to enrage the people as much as did the adoption of the "Ironclad Oath" requirement placed in the new constitution. It declared that any Missourian *"who had ever been in armed hostility to the United States"* or *"has ever given aid, comfort, countenance or support to persons engaged in any such hostility,*" or "*has ever disloyally held communication with such enemies*" could not vote.[136] Essentially this "*Oath of Loyalty*" served as a "*document of revenge*" upon southern sympathizers.[137] It declared over eighty personal actions as evidence of disloyalty.[138] Under this law a father who sent food or clothing to a son who served under the Confederate flag lost his right to vote. A non-combatant Missourian who tended to the wounds of his rebel brother lost the vote. Even though women couldn't vote, some were teachers. A teacher whose betrothed served in a southern army might lose her job. And so on…. This effectively prohibited any pro-Southern support for any candidate in any election in the state. Many would have supported a simple requirement for former pro-South Missourians to take an oath of allegiance from that point onward. There had already been a similar oath requirement at the beginning of the Civil War. Fletcher had strongly supported it during his term as Deputy Provost Marshal in St. Louis. This "weak" oath did not satisfy Drake or the other Radical Republicans. They wanted a "*pound of flesh.*"

The so called "*Iron Clad Oath*" had other consequences besides limitation of rights related to voting and holding office. The actual impact on lawyers, teachers, political leaders, and even ministers and Catholic priests proved to be inflammatory at best. The *St. Louis News* took the stand that "*no loyal minister can have any scruples about taking the oath. A minister refusing to take it gives conclusive evidence of his disloyalty and should not preach the Gospel in this or any other State. The Gospel is the very essence of loyalty. Obedience to the laws, rendering unto Caesar the things that are Caesar's and obeying the powers that be, are fundamental principles of the Gospel, and the minister who fails to regard them as such should be stripped of his ermine.*"[139] Perhaps most of the clergy did not agree with this sentiment. Even Frank Blair disagreed with the requirement. And Fletcher did not find anything about the Ironclad Oath agreeable. But it really didn't matter what he felt. He had to enforce the law—this abominable law as well as any other duly passed by the State legislature.

---

[136] Meyer, *Heritage of Missouri*, 408.

[137] Ibid.

[138] Parrish, *History of Missouri, Vol. III,* 121.

[139] as quoted in *The Howard Union* (Glasgow, Missouri), August 10, 1865, 4.

Fletcher strongly opposed this constitution in general but particularly this odious section. While he worked with the legislature as best as possible and seldom took a vocal stance against their actions, he felt this law jeopardized religious freedom and went way too far. He finally just could not remain silent. In one speech in October, 1865, He noted,

> There is an old Gaelic proverb which says that 'he that will not look before him must look behind him.' This truth has been made manifest in the cases of some of our friends, who, having been swift to adopt the new constitution, have since, for want of other pretext, discovered that there is an unconstitutional abridgement of religious liberty in the provision of that instrument that requires an oath of loyalty from ministers of the gospel.[140]

While willing to publicly express his disappointment and disgust with parts of the new constitution, he did not mount a significant campaign against it. To do so might result in further destabilization of the government and further divide the populace. At this time, the state leadership needed to be seen as speaking with one voice. Probably biting his tongue, the young governor turned his focus to other pressing issues; even distasteful ones.

One of his first difficult and probably very uncomfortable actions was to remove, by force if necessary, two sitting State Supreme Court justices. The Ousting Ordinance required this. The noncompliant justices had visibly ignored the law although their offices were only a block from the state capital building where Fletcher worked. This very visible opposition had to be dealt with. About ten o'clock on the morning of On June 12, 1865, General D. C. Coleman, of the enrolled militia, walked into the Missouri Supreme Court, interrupting the proceedings. Fletcher had issued him an order, "*Brig. Gen. D. C. Coleman is charged with the executing the [ouster] order and will employ such force for that purpose as he may deem necessary and arrest all persons who may oppose him.*"[141] The sitting justices

---

[140] *Missouri State Times* (Jefferson City, Missouri), October 27, 1865.
[141] *Missouri State Times,* June 16, 1865, 1.

had not vacated their positions as required by the Ousting Ordinance and were going about their normal business. Just a few lawyers and clerks were in the courtroom as the scheduled trial had not commenced. The general's entrance made quite a jarring site. Coleman had served in the Army of the Tennessee with Fletcher and had the governor's complete confidence; deservedly so. After a brief, but probably heated discussion and seeing ten armed men waiting in the hallway, the judges left the building peacefully with General Coleman—but did so reluctantly.[142] As far away as Alexandria, Virginia, the removal of Justices John D.S. Driden and W.V.N. Bay as they actually sat on the bench at the Missouri Supreme Court building made headlines.[143] Across Missouri the action made all those who sat in targeted positions take notice. Most became resigned to the removal from their respective jobs. Of course, some vowed to vacate only if forced. That would be arranged.

Across the state other public officials were removed; some by force or at least with the presence of nearby armed militia. Some pro-Southern office holders, ironically or not, were escorted out of office by professional black militia recruited by the governor. This, of course, did not go over well in most out-state jurisdictions. The Ousting Ordinance resulted in many vacant seats but also facilitated the slow recovery of a mostly effective justice system, even if tempered by Radical Republican ideology. The governor's specially selected troops met resistance with determination but attempted not to be inflammatory. Most of the time they were successful.

The Ouster Ordinance eventually dissipated as the offices were reclaimed or established through the regular electoral process—also vigorously protected by Fletcher. The U. S. Supreme Court, however, later nullified the Ironclad Oath but not before much damage had occurred.

Fletcher continued to enforce these and other laws he hated. One of his guiding principles centered on the need for respect for the law. He knew that this had to originate from the top—him. If the chief executive of the state selectively enforced laws it wouldn't be much different from

---

[142] *Washington Telegraph* (Washington, Arkansas) July 5, 1865, 1.
[143] *Alexandria Gazette,* (Alexandria, Virginia) October 7, 1865, 2.

the anarchy that existed in outstate Missouri. If the people knew that *all* laws were enforced, they might understand that their own safety would also be assured. Fletcher also understood the principle of "Separation of Powers" as it applied to state government. The three branches had different responsibilities. The Governor had to enforce the laws. The legislature passed the laws. The Judiciary reviewed the laws for constitutionality and served as arbiter in some situations. Fletcher looked to the state and federal judiciary to correct the egregious error made by the legislature in its passage of several odious sections of the new constitution. Until that occurred, however, his duty became clear to all—enforce the law. That he did.

Just a few weeks into the convention the new governor turned thirty-eight years old. He faced a monumental task ahead—to restore the state: economically, socially, and politically. And he would have to do so in a war zone that had not been completely pacified.

Missouri at the End of the War

The state Fletcher now led exemplified all that could be devastating in any war-torn population. Some estimated that over twenty-seven thousand civilians had lost their lives during the war in the outstate Missouri counties.[144] Federal troops had defeated the last remnants of Price's army before the end of 1864, but Guerrilla leader William Quantrill had merely retreated into Kentucky, possibly to return at some point. "Bloody Bill" Anderson had been killed a month after his September, 1864, massacre of unarmed troops and civilians outside of Centralia, Missouri. Frank and Jesse James, Cole Younger, and other "guerrillas" were temporarily thwarted by the Federal troops and State Militia. Still, isolated violence constantly erupted as Tom Fletcher assumed office. Less than a month after Lee surrendered, guerrilla Archie Clement unsuccessfully demanded the surrender of Lexington, Missouri.[145] Outlaw Sam Hildebrand still roamed and killed at will as Fletcher began his term and the legislature met in Jefferson City. Southern supporters took out frustrations on northern sympathizer neighbors. Northern supporters often would have nothing to do with their former neighbors returning from tours of duty in the mostly defeated

---

[144] Paul Nagel, *Missouri: A History*, (W.W. Norton & Company, New York, 1977). 128.
[145] While the city did not surrender, "little Arch" continued to harass the area until Fletcher's militia killed him in December, 1866. One of his men escaped— Jesse James.

Confederacy. Or, they would turn to violence. Fear reigned across the state and outstate Missourians fitfully slept with their guns loaded and placed conveniently nearby. They sometimes needed them.

Missouri slaveholders had lost their livelihoods due to the loss of their labor source—slaves. In fact, then entire state suffered from lack of labor. Many sons, brothers and husbands did not return from the war. Produce often rotted in the fields. Even if crops could be harvested, getting them to market became a real challenge, brigands notwithstanding. Railroads did not operate due to wartime sabotage and lack of new roadbed construction. Bridges had been destroyed on many major roadways. The lives of outstate citizens were "iffy" at best. The families suffered and feared for their children's futures. Their lives were complicated by Missouri's general instability.

Few schools operated outside of the larger cities. Banks which had supported Southerners found themselves without financial support and became bankrupt themselves. Law and order had, in many areas, reverted to "vigilance committees." The justice received in many counties depended upon the whims of whatever county judges and sheriffs were in office. The state university served as barracks for federal troops and meeting places for militia. Prices of all commodities had risen due to scarcity:

St. Louis, Missouri Cost of Living— 1860-1865 compared:

		1860	1865
Tobacco, 100lbs	$	10.50	85.00
Bacon, hams lb		9	19.50
Corn, bushel		50	68
Coffee, Rio, lb		16.50	32.50
Cheese, lb		10	22
Eggs, doz		7	35
Flour, bbl.		5	12.50
Wheat, bushel		1.20	2.60
Apples, green, bbl.		1.25	4

Peaches, dried, bushel	2	6.75
Feathers, pound	41	90
Hemp, ton	120	285
Lard, lb	13	33
Whiskey	.18	2.27
sugar, lb	8.50	17.75
Potatoes, Irish, bushel	44	75
Onions, bushel	35	60
Beef cattle, lb gross	2.75	7
hogs, lb, gross	6.50	12
sheep, per head	3	6.50

Much of the outstate citizenry had reverted to barter in order to feed their families. Farmers who lived near populated areas took their goods to market to obtain currency but feared the possibility of robbers along the roads; a not infrequent occurrence. They did their best to help their neighbors—at least the ones with whom they were aligned. After harvesting their own crops, many farmers then rode over to their neighbors to help them. Shortages of labor on one farm were filled as best as possible by the closest friends. But, many of the outstate farms were no longer even in operation. The families had fled.

The four counties vacated by General Ewing (Jackson, Cass, Bates and Vernon) were still mostly empty as Fletcher took office. About twenty thousand families had been displaced in this attempt to prevent guerilla resupply.[147] Some had attempted to temporarily locate nearby but others simply left almost everything they had in the homestead hoping to return at some point. Many could not return; most likely did not want to. Throughout the outstate area, Federal troops and State Militia still patrolled but seldom arrived in time to prevent bloodshed and property destruction at flash points. Grief permeated the populace due to the death of family members whose bodies were never recovered due to horrendous battlefield conditions. Hundreds of unknown, often mutilated bodies

---

[146] *The Howard Union* (Glasgow, Missouri), November 23, 1865, 1.
[147] Duane Schultz, *Quantrill's War,* St Martin's Griffin (New York), 1996, 243-44.

were thrown on top of each other in mass burials near a battlefield or placed in shallow graves. Prior to the war, families had some closure when a loved-one died. The body was reverently washed, dressed, honored, and often buried on the family farm in the presence of the grieving family, friends and the local church leaders. Churches seemed helpless to offer comfort and many Missourians suffered a crisis of faith. The catastrophic conditions in Missouri came to the attention of the White House and Missouri's critical situation seemed to offer implications for the future in the other Southern states that were to be "reconstructed." In February, 1865, President Lincoln and the new young governor Thomas Fletcher exchanged letters. The president wrote:

> …It seems that there is no organized military force of the country in Missouri and that destruction of property and life is rampant everywhere. Is not the cure for this within easy reach of the people themselves? It cannot but be that every man, not naturally a robber or cutthroat would gladly put an end to this state of things. A large majority in every locality must feel alike upon this subject; and they only need to reach an understanding one with another. Each leaving all others alone solves the problem.; and surely each would do this but for his apprehension that other will not leave him alone. Cannot this mischievous distrust be removed? Let neighborhood meetings be everywhere called and held, of all entertaining sincere purpose for mutual security in the future, whatever they man heretofore have thought said or done about the war or about anything else,
>
> Let all such meet, and waiving all else, pledge each to cease harassing others, and to make common cause against whomsoever persists in making, aiding or encouraging further disturbance. The practical means that they will best know how to adopt and apply. At such meetings old friendships will cross the memory, and honor and Christian charity will come in to help.

Please consider whether it may not be well to suggest this
to the now afflicted people of Missouri.[148]

This letter from the president to Governor Fletcher became a national issue. The *Philadelphia Enquirer* reprinted the letter and noted that the *Republican* newspaper had also presented it to the people. Other papers followed suit and published it—inside the state and across the nation. The future of Missouri concerned everyone in America. All probably feared what might happen to other areas like Missouri that might have adjustment difficulties after the war.[149] If the transition to normalcy worked in this war-torn state, the other Southern states might also have hope. The president really believed in the *"greater angels"* of people's nature as he had stated in his first inaugural address.

Fletcher greatly admired and respected President Lincoln. He could legitimately describe Lincoln as a friend. Receiving this missive probably caused the governor great internal conflict. Being a formal military man, Fletcher understood the role of Commander in Chief held by the president. The president needed to be listened to. In some ways, this "suggestion" could be considered an order. Still early in his tenure of office as governor, Fletcher's role as governor in a state under federal occupation with presidential oversight led to questions about what he should do. There were also political concerns; local and nationally. Of course, he wanted to keep the friendship with Lincoln and he really needed the support of the President of the United States. He knew the weight of the world sat on Lincoln's shoulders. Returning the nation to some semblance of normality would take massive effort on national, state and local levels. Lincoln surely had the skills to guide the nation, Tom believed. And, Fletcher hoped he could emulate them himself.

Lincoln's faith in "everyman," while laudable did not appear very perceptive, the young governor also thought. Few people really

---

[148] Governor's Correspondence, Missouri State Archives, Finding Aid 3.18; note: due to a 1911 fire in the State Archives most of Fletcher's papers were destroyed. According to tradition, he and Lincoln had significant positive contact. Likely, these additional papers were destroyed.

[149] *Philadelphia Enquirer* (Philadelphia, Pennsylvania), April 6, 1865, 4.

understood the terrible situation in the state. In many ways, Missouri citizens might have been worse off than those living in many Southern states. In the South, the white people seldom worried about their white neighbors' antagonism. They did not fear that a neighbor might kill them or sneak over in the middle of the night and burn the family barn. Southern white population remained cohesive even through military occupation. At least a clear point of demarcation existed in Southern states once the fighting ended. With the ending of the war, reconstruction could begin. However, the civil war might continue in Missouri even after the South surrendered and national peace returned. Reconciliation in Missouri seemed in the distant future, if at any time. The lawlessness in the border state really existed to that extent when the president's letter arrived at the governor's mansion. With the mutual distrust and enmity still boiling over in Missouri, calm neighborhood meetings across the state seemed unlikely. Fletcher carefully crafted his own response to the president's letter which he considered to be a bit naïve. Governor Fletcher's letter addressed the President with grace but realistic clarity:

> *Trusting that I have that full knowledge of the subject of your communication, and have given it that thought, which its importance to the people of my state demands, I have to say: that the destruction of life and property in every part of Missouri which has been going on for nearly four years, and which is yet going on, it is not the result of the immediate action of men who can be reached by amicable propositions. The state being infected by thousands of outlaws who are naturally and practically "robbers" and "cutthroats," no good man desires to reach any understanding with them or to enter into any agreement or leave them alone…. No theatre of this war has presented scenes of murder and outrage such as we have witnessed in Missouri…. A whole neighborhood of forty or fifty peaceable farmers have been murdered in a single day while quietly pursuing their vocations—men sick in bed and men ninety years old included in the wholesale butchery.*

I am satisfied, Mr. President, that if you could see and fully understand what we have done and suffered in Missouri for the cause of the Union, you would agree with me that we want no peace with rebels but the peace which comes of unconditional submission to the authority of the law.

I am just now organizing, under a militia law recently enacted, all the able men of the state. ... our troops will remedy much of the wrong and injury experienced by our people....

I will inform [the military] of the subject of your letter.... I will... confer with Pope and Dodge as to the best method of fully testing the policy suggested by you, and in earnest hope that I may be mistaken as to the result.... I will go into the districts where the greatest trouble exists; will talk to the people and in good faith labor for its success, meanwhile preparing for consequences of its failure. I must candidly admit... the only desirable peace with [the murderers and cutthroats] is the peace which will come of their extermination....

The constitutional convention... [will make] ...the side of loyalty the only side of safety.[150]

Fletcher began to make plans to follow Lincoln's suggestions and asked his cabinet and a few friends to think about how that could be accomplished. But, there were many other issues in the days ahead and this fell to the back burner—or was pushed there. Of course, within a few days after the receipt of this letter the president visited Ford's Theater attempting to get some relaxation.

There were serious regional issues that also affected Fletcher's Missouri. Even though Kansas had entered the Union in 1861, it still resembled more of a wilderness than a state at the end of the war. The western part of Kansas had few soldiers available to keep the Native-Americans in check. Troops continuously crossed Missouri to get to or

---

[150] Ibid.

return from attempting to protect trails to Santa Fe, Oregon or California. Traders also initiated their western journeys in western Missouri, often after buying goods near Kansas City or the St. Joseph area. This posed some positive financial possibilities for the state. But westward travel had become far less safe during the war. The Native-Americans west of Missouri used this opportunity to rebel against the white intrusions. Most tribes really liked the idea of whites killing whites during the Civil War. The removal of Federal troops from the west gave encouragement to the angry Native-Americans. The American Southwest reeled from Apache, Navaho and Comanche bloody resistance. In 1861, a large section of Arizona lost almost ninety-percent of the male population due to Native-American attacks.[151] Those whites crossing the Great Plains, particularly the northern part, found Sioux, Cheyenne, Arapahos, Crows and others resistant to their movements. In 1862 a Dakota Sioux uprising in Minnesota occurred as a result of the Federal government not honoring their existent treaty. The Union Army had other issues to deal with and Indian rights were just not a high priority; or a priority at all. Ruthlessly defeating the uprising, angry about the hundreds of settlers killed, and perhaps also angry about the loss at the Second Battle of Bull Run, the authorities sentenced over three-hundred Dakota captives to be hanged for alleged (and actual) atrocities. Thirty-eight were actually hanged on a specially-built gallows.[152] Their cadavers were dug up and eventually used for medical purposes. Even in California the Modocs and other indigenous tribes presented difficulties to the white desire for their elimination. Missouri businessmen were reluctant to commit a large amount of resources to almost any western speculation; especially without sufficient troops to ensure safety.

Even before the Civil War, the Federal troops that patrolled the over one million square miles in the West seldom numbered over eight thousand. Even these were undersupplied and poorly trained. Many had never fired a weapon and did not have the opportunity to learn much while billeted in the west. Bullets were expensive so target practice

---

[151] John Tebbel, *The Compact History of the Indian Wars*, (Tower Publications, Inc., New York, 1966), 191.

[152] This was the largest mass execution in United States history.

seldom occurred *(many of Custer's men had fired their own rifle less than a dozen times)*. Regardless of training or natural ability, the soldiers had to perform arduous and dangerous duties. They were spread loosely along the westward trails. Peace had depended upon agreements like the famous Fort Laramie Treaty of 1851 where famous mountain man and scout, Jim Bridger, and Governor Fletcher's friend, Robert Campbell, helped draw the tribal borders for the western tribes. The Civil War drew many of the western troops eastward—to Union or Confederate brigades. This left the western settlers and Native-Americans living in a tinder-box. The 1864 massacre of peaceful Cheyenne villagers at Sand Creek by the Colorado Militia *"reverberated among the tribes of the region and touched off a general war for the Plains. The Cheyenne and Arapaho allied with the Sioux to assault white settlements across Colorado. A force of a thousand Indians... [destroyed]...the village of Jonesburg."*[153] The Sioux leader, Red Cloud, proved to be a determined and formidable foe. Missouri businessmen ventured westward at their own risk; commerce almost came to a stand-still during the war and immediately thereafter.

By the time Fletcher became governor, the *"Indian Territory"* (today called Oklahoma) lying to the southwest of the state provided poor land but a peaceful residence for the tribes who had once lived east of the Mississippi River. There were many, especially Cherokee, who aligned themselves with either the North or the South and actively fought in the war. But, in general, the pacification of this area had been successful— unlike in the Great Plains. But the area also provided safe haven for outlaws who raided Missouri and then fled back to Indian Territory.

Even the Confederate government recognized the importance of alliances with the Native-Americans. They had successfully negotiated a peace treaty accepted by many western tribes and thus endangered the Western Federal supporters. Of course, after the war, the Confederate-Native-American treaty had no validity. Also, after the war, many whites had flocked into the west and could not have cared less about treaties. One of the first efforts to protect western trails after the war centered

---

[153] H.W. Brands, *The Man Who Saved the Union; Ulysses Grant in War and Peace*, Doubleday (New York), 2012, 411.

at the newly named Fort Fletcher, later moved a quarter of a mile and renamed Fort Hays, and then just Hays, Kansas. The federal troops were supposed to protect the Butterfield Stage Line operating from Missouri to Denver. Opened in October,1865, by the middle of 1866 the fort had proved ineffectual. Too many Indians, too expansive geography and too few soldiers. The military found itself with the unenviable responsibility of honoring the treaties, keeping the trails safe for those crossing the Indian territory and keeping unscrupulous white opportunists from stealing gold, horses or anything else of value, or killing and robbing Native-Americans.

While these western complications certainly concerned Fletcher, the first responsibility of the governor certainly had to be the safety of his own population inside his own state. This, in no way, seemed to be an easy task. He didn't have any effective state-operated fighting force. He needed a large militia and began a massive and largely successful recruitment effort. While his new militia forces were being prepared, the Federal forces had to hold on. Shortly after the inauguration, General John Pope, commander of the Northern forces in Missouri, encouraged the governor's efforts and believed the state would be under control in a relative short time.[154] His optimism proved premature. But the surrender of General Robert E. Lee to General Ulysses S. Grant on April 9th at Appomattox, Virginia, brought pause to all concerned. The war effectively ended after this event—although "some mopping up" still remained. The last battles or skirmishes ended by the end of May and the last Confederate Brigadier-General, Stand Watie, surrendered in June.[155] Many Confederates, Sterling Price, Joe Shelby, John Magruder, fled to Mexico in unsuccessful attempts to join the forces of Maximillian and/or to establish a home for exiles. Thus, they effected no continuing hostilities in the United States. But it was November before the last Confederate naval ship surrendered.

Fletcher, the legislature, and especially those living in the St. Louis area rejoiced at the end of the war. They held celebrations, made speeches, and looked forward to the world returning to something near normal.

---

[154] *The Pittsburgh Daily Commercial* (Pittsburgh, Pennsylvania), March 9, 1865,1.

[155] Stand Watie was a Cherokee Indian who commanded the Confederate Indian cavalry of the Army of the Trans-Mississippi, consisting of Cherokee, Muskogee and Seminole.

Lincoln held the key to the Reconstruction of the nation. Even Southerners felt Lincoln might be reasonable; well, at least many Southerners believed that. The assassination of President Abraham Lincoln on April 15th, however, placed everything on hold and created a national trauma.

The death of his friend hit the governor hard. Fletcher led the Missouri delegation to Springfield, Illinois, for the funeral services on a special train accompanied by about three hundred people.[156] Mourning continued after the burial as the impact of the president's death began to set in. Fletcher declared June 1, 1865 as a day of "*fasting, humiliation and prayer throughout the state... as expression of sorrow over the assassination of the late loved and honored Chief Magistrate.*"[157]

But, even during the time of mourning for Lincoln and the uneasy transition of power to Andrew Johnson, Governor Fletcher had to keep focusing on the issues in Missouri.

---

[156] *The St. Louis Star and Times* (St. Louis, Missouri, February 12, 1934, 3.
[157] Giffen, *First Ladies of Missouri,* 91.

The Governor Begins Reconstruction

For the remainder of his term of office, law and order remained priority number one. His first efforts which had included the use of Federal forces to protect the people and dissuade armed groups of bushwhackers were successful. State Militia Patrols were increased and military efficiency improved through continuous recruitment and effective training. The second effort, the establishment of an effective militia to act as interim peace keepers in areas not controlled by the federal government, also had been effective. Governor Fletcher intentionally recruited former slaves; especially former black soldiers. These well-trained and eager black troops that had performed many of the "ouster" functions also patrolled the countryside as needed. These men, much to the chagrin of the former slaveholders or Southern supporters, increased stability in the state. Fletcher continually recruited other responsible civilians to join the militia. A not-so-unintended consequence, providing funding for many men, helped revitalize the economy. The enrollment for the militia continued throughout his term, sometimes more aggressively than others. After a particularly difficult few months in late1866, his frustration almost leapt off the paper he published a proclamation on in December,

A portion of the State of Missouri is infested with
murderers and robbers who defy the civil authority and have

*the sympathy and aid of a number of counties where they
have their haunts, and have so intimidated or obtained the
sympathy of the local authorities that peaceable and law-
abiding citizens are not secure in their person or property;
therefore I, Thomas Fletcher, Governor do call upon the
people of the State to volunteer by companies as enrolled
in the militia to the number of twenty-four companies of
cavalry and ten companies of infantry, to be organized and
to proceed under my orders, as the chief executive officer of
the State, to preserve the peace and protect the citizens of
the State in their persons and property, and to institute legal
process on all violations of the law, and bring them to trial.*

He had the volunteers trained and assigned them tasks as needed
for the remainder of his governorship. It worked; but not without some
very vocal criticism—especially from racist former Confederates and
rebel sympathizers. Many of his supporters feared for the governor's life
and urged a stepped-up security. Fletcher refused and traveled mostly
unaccompanied by any armed escorts throughout his term of office.[158]

The Missouri citizenry had been used to taking things into their
own hands during the war; often with disastrous results. Vigilance
committees had sprung up across the state, especially in areas where
the legal authorities were biased or ineffectual. Perhaps remembering
Lincoln's words about getting people to come together, in July, 1865, only
three months after the assassination, Fletcher suggested, *"We must return
to the process of the law, to the peaceful remedies of the law, to the spirit of
forgiveness and fraternity so honorable to our nature and so essential to the
interests of society."*[159] But, the state continued to reel from lawlessness. In
August 1865, newspapers carried the story of a forty-member vigilance
committee in Benton County that took a bushwhacker named John Hill
from the sheriff and riddled the outlaw with over thirty bullets.[160] In
the early fall of 1866 dozens of newspapers across the nation reported

---

[158] *Harrisburg Telegraph* (Harrisburg, Pennsylvania), December 12, 1866, 2,
[159] *The Howard Union,* July 20, 1865, 3.
[160] *The Holt County Sentinel* (Oregon, Missouri), August 4, 1865, 3.

on shootings in Kansas City, Independence, and elsewhere in western Missouri occurring within a few days of each other. An incredible event of lawlessness in Platte County, Missouri, in September that same year, perhaps gave illustration of the continuing tensions between northern and southern sympathizers. The *Philadelphia Enquirer* briefly summarized the events:

> *After the adjournment of the Platte County Radical Convention…a drunken Union soldier, named Donnegan, made some noise on the street, and flourished a pistol about considerably.*
>
> *Sheriff Ogden took his pistol away and told him to keep quiet, which he did. Shortly afterwards a returned Rebel…with a posse of ten men, demanded the surrender of Donnegan. A scuffle ensued and pistols were freely used, resulting in the death of three or four and the wounding of eight or ten men.*
>
> *A number of delegates, who had started for home… returned to town and were fired on….*
>
> *The latest accounts say, that several hundred armed Rebels hold Platte City and have driven all the Union men out of town, and swear they shall not return.*
>
> *Great excitement prevails. Governor Fletcher has been appealed to for a force to put down the mob….*[161]

Even as late as 1867, readers learned about two hundred vigilantes in Johnson County who took two horse thieves from the sheriff and killed them.[162] Another, more colorful and illuminating report came from an outstate paper reporting about an event near Kansas City

> *… Dick Sanders, the notorious desperado, "The Knight of Four Revolvers," was found hung by the neck from a tree, in the immediate vicinity of the late murder, he being, as*

---

[161] *Philadelphia Inquirer,* (Philadelphia, Pennsylvania), September 18, 1866, 1.

[162] *Harrisburg Telegraph* (Harrisburg, Pennsylvania), May 25, 1867, 2.

rumor says, captured in the house of his brother-in-law, by a posse of over sixty men, some of whom identifies him as one of the murderers of Mr. Switzer on Monday last. Sanders made no confession, but enough was obtained from him to show he belonged to a gang of thieves and desperadoes whose late exploits of murder and horse stealing have created so much terror in this and adjoining counties.... Great excitement exists in the vicinity, and a large mass meeting was held in the court house yesterday afternoon, participated in by persons of all parties, and a determination was come to immediately form vigilance committees throughout the county and western part of the state. Among those who are at the head of the committee are men who were prominent in the committee at San Francisco, California in 1858.[163]

Such "law-enforcement" had become common and hard to rein in. The simple fact was that law and order had broken down in many western Missouri counties. Outlaws roamed at will, often supported by local citizenry. Knowing that unusual times took unusual methods, Fletcher also used unorthodox means such as proclamations:

WHEREAS OUR STATE IS STILL infested with murderers and outlaws who have heretofore eluded the vigilance of the civil and military authorities, and

Whereas, foremost among the stands one Samuel Hildebrand, a notorious brigand and murderer....and

Whereas, This said Samuel Hildebrand is still at large....

Now, therefore, I Thomas C. Fletcher, Governor of the State of Missouri...hereby offer a reward of three hundred dollars (about $4,200 in 2018 dollars), for the arrest and deliver of the body of the said Samuel Hildebrand, either to the civil or military authorities at Pilot Knob or Farmington, Missouri.[164]

---

[163] *Harrisburg Telegraph* (Harrisburg, Pennsylvania) March 2, 1867,1.

[164] *Weekly Arkansas Gazette* (Little Rock, Arkansas), June 24, 1865, Proclamation; note: Hildebrand was later killed by an Illinois marshal in 1872.

Fletcher knew that lawlessness affected everyone—rebel or Unionist. Those who came back from fighting for the South had to start new lives. They faced not only outlaws but also angry and suspicious neighbors. As early as July, 1865, the new governor lamented the treatment of returning rebels being forced away from homes *"not by Federal soldiers, but by stay-at-home citizens who probably show by these outrages on defenseless men that they are actuated by the same cowardice which kept them out of the ranks of the army.: 'Our soldiers were too brave to be cruel or vindictive to an armed foe; too heroic to take vengeance on soldiers who had surrendered....'"* The war was over and large numbers of rebel soldiers were returning to our midst, he went on to say. *"Let us stand in good faith with the National Government, and by the doctrine of leniency and fraternity."* He continued to explain that the state needs *"all the inhabitants she can get...."*[165] There were those who listened and those who didn't. And the new constitution complicated the relationships between people.

Resistance to the provisions of the Constitution increased and Fletcher used the anger toward the Ironclad Oath to explain his duty,

> *...the provisions of the Constitution requiring an oath of ministers and teachers, are to be construed by the courts.*
>
> *Any question as to the right of the people...will be for the higher judicial tribunals of the country to determine. Pending their decision, the law must be regarded as valid and of binding force.*
>
> *My action in enforcing these and all other laws will be strictly within the scope of the legal powers conferred on me, and I shall require on the part of all citizens, that their acts in giving force to this law will be done in the legal manner.*
>
> *...The whole military forces of the State will be at the command of the officers of the law, to enforce legal processes....*
>
> *The Constitution in all its provisions, is the highest law of the State... all the duties devolved upon the Executive by*

---

[165] *The Howard Union* (Glasgow, Missouri), July 20, 1865, 3.

law for enforcing it, will be, in due time and in a proper manner, fully performed.[166]

Fletcher understood the nature of the office of Chief Executive and felt committed to ethically perform his duties—regardless of whether he agreed with the requirements or not. At the same time, he encouraged the General Assembly to submit a constitutional amendment that would repeal the oath for lawyers, teachers, and ministers. These Draconian laws, he felt, were unnecessary and ones that fed anarchy.[167] He earnestly told the state citizens, *"Let our laws be just and wise, let them be few and plain."*[168]

But Fletcher did not just blindly follow laws. When an injustice came to his attention he tried to correct it. When famous Irish Mountain man and St. Louis Entrepreneur Robert Campbell asked him to review the case of Michael Williams, Campbell's close friend, the governor complied with the request. The pardon came through less than three weeks after the request had been received in Jefferson City.[169] During the last two years of his term Fletcher also issued four hundred and nineteen pardons to penitentiary inmates and *"complimented returned rebels for the orderly manner in which they behaved since they returned.*[170] These actions drew attention across the South; and probably confused those who looked negatively toward his administration.[171] When he did not have the authority to pardon someone he felt deserved a second chance, he appealed directly to President Johnson,

Charles R. Jones, who was convicted in the U.S. District Court for Eastern District of Mo for having counterfeit money in his possession and who is now confined in the Mo

---

[166] *The Howard Union* (Glasgow, Missouri), September 7, 1865, 2.

[167] Parrish, *Missouri Under Radical Rule*, 73-74.

[168] *The Holt County Sentinel* (Oregon, Missouri), November 17, 1865, 2.

[169] Robert Campbell to Thomas Fletcher, March 1, 1866; Hugh Campbell to Michael Williams, March 23, 1866, 1866 Letterbook, Mercantile Library, St. Louis, Missouri.

[170] *Nashville Union and American* (Nashville, Tennessee), January 12, 1869, 1.

[171] *Richmond Dispatch*, April 10, 1867. 3.

Penitentiary is a young man and I am informed and believe that this is his first offence. His conduct as to (unintelligible) is favorably stated to me by the warden. If he produces evidence satisfactory to you of a (unintelligible) character I recommend that he be pardoned.[172]

Like Lincoln, Fletcher still believed that a normal state of interaction between former combatants could eventually be developed in Missouri. At some time, punishment had to stop and reconciliation begin. He even released noted architect and construction engineer James B Eads' from prosecution related to an assault charge.[173] Fletcher provided an equal and fair administration of justice for Missouri. He listened to the people.

For the entirety of his term. Fletcher received pleas to protect elections, provide general security from violence and bring outlaws and bushwhackers to justice. It became so difficult in late December of 1866 he declared martial law in certain counties,

A portion of the State of Missouri is infested with murderers and robbers who defy the civil authority and have the sympathy and aid of a number of the countries were they have their haunts, and have so intimidated or obtained the sympathy of the local authorities that peaceable and law-abiding citizens are not secure in their persons and property; Therefore I, Thomas Fletcher, Governor, do call upon the people of the State to volunteer by companies, as enrolled in the militia, to the number of twenty-four companies of cavalry and ten companies of infantry, to be organized and to proceed under my orders, as the chief executive officer of the State, to preserve the peace and protect the citizens of

---

[172] Thomas Fletcher, Letter to the President, October 6, 1868, Missouri Historical Society. Fletcher Collection.

[173] *Executive Order of Governor Thomas C. Fletcher*, releasing James B. Eads from prosecution, January 6, 1865, Missouri Historical Society Archives, St. Louis, Missouri.

the State in their persons and property, and to institute legal
process on all violations of the law, and bring them to trial.[174]

At times Fletcher actually went to the disaffected area and took personal command of the militia. His military experience came in handy when this course of action had been decided upon. In Lafayette County, he put on his military uniform and adjusted the perimeters of the occupation, removing militia from Jackson County as he deemed the county functioning satisfactorily. He also warned counties that any military occupation would be at their expense until they could demonstrate return to civil law.[175] Hitting noncompliant rebels in their pocketbook or just threatening to do so proved an effective and non-lethal tactic. Fletcher continued to believe Missouri could handle its own problems without occupying federal forces—eventually. His tactics, while often unappreciated in parts of Missouri, gained national attention. The Virginia newspaper, *Staunton Spectator* accused Fletcher as "... *secretly organizing the negroes of St. Louis in order to have a force which may overcome the whites... to insure a disciplined corps of semi-barbarians to assist in reducing free citizens to a state of slavery....*"[176] On a more positive side, Maryland announced in early November 1866, that they would imitate Governor Fletcher's militia-based law enforcement system.[177] By his last day in office the federal forces had effectively left the state except for small contingencies. Regardless, the state still had isolated pockets of violence. Jesse James had returned to the state.

---

[174] *Harrisburg Telegraph* (Harrisburg, Pennsylvania), December 12, 1866, 2.
[175] *The Holt County Sentinel* (Oregon, Missouri), November 17, 1865, 2; *The Louisville Daily Courier* (Louisville, Kentucky), December 14, 1866, 4; *Detroit Free Press* (Detroit, Michigan), December 21, 1866 · Page 8; *Daily Ohio Statesman* (Columbus, Ohio), December 22, 1866, 3.
[176] *Staunton Spectator* (Staunton, Virginia), August 14, 1866, 2.
[177] *Richmond Dispatch* (Richmond, Virginia), November 16, 1866, 3.

Fletcher Aids Black Missourians

Among the many other areas of concern to Fletcher during his term, the critical issue of how to deal with Freedmen stood out. Improving the lives of black Missourians had been the main reason he enlisted in the military. In fact, this commitment shaped his life at the time. As governor, Fletcher might be able to achieve his goals. Certainly, the Emancipation Proclamation advanced the effort. But, the franchise eluded the black population—and Fletcher's efforts to secure it for them. The popular attitude toward freed slaves varied across the state. Many encouraged full franchise. Fletcher agreed. Others wanted gradual franchise. The Southern supporters, of course, wanted no black franchise at all—ever. There were some who even wanted freed slaves expunged from the state. "Loyal" slave owners wanted compensation; they eventually did get some funds as opposed to the pro-Southern slave holders whose losses were never even partially compensated.

But there were other needs among the state's black population, perhaps more basic even than the vote. Food, shelter, clothing, and education were some of the essential requirements for any future success of any kind. A large part of the white population wanted educational institutions to improve for the benefit of all children; including the former slaves. Fletcher successfully supported the effort to improve educational opportunities in Missouri. He knew what his own education had allowed him to accomplish. A significant group that believed that freedom had been obtained for the former slaves; that would be as far as they would go. Issues related to full political, legal, economic and social equality did not receive much attention from any white Missourians. At least one of these issues was solved shortly after Fletcher left office when the Fifteenth Amendment became part of the constitution giving black males the right to vote. It would be over a hundred and fifty years before many of the other issues were even close to being resolved in Missouri.[178] Many remained a large question-mark in the state in the early twenty-first century. Fletcher, however, remained committed to full equality for black Americans throughout his term of office and for the rest of his life.

Initially, even during the last part of the war, the Freedmen's Bureau had helped thousands of black Americans across the nation. The Bureau of Refugees, Freedmen and Abandoned Lands (popularly called "Freedmen's Bureau") came into existence in March, 1865. It *"managed all matters relating to refugees, freedmen, and lands abandoned or seized by Federal authorities during the Civil War. Providing relief and assistance to freedmen, the Bureau issued rations and clothing, operated hospitals and refugee camps, and supervised labor contracts. It also managed apprenticeship disputes, assisted in the establishment of schools, helped former slaves legalize their marriages, and provided transportation to refugees and freedmen."*[179] It had been very active in Missouri and remained so for a short time after Fletcher took office. Between June, 1865, and September, 1866, 1,705,055 rations were distributed in Missouri to a hundred refugees and over fifteen thousand freedmen. The new governor worked closely with the Bureau. But by the end of 1868 the program had mostly ended in Missouri, attributed partially due to the effective legal system repaired by Fletcher.[180] Under the governor's economic development efforts, the lives of black Missourians improved slightly and the law protected their limited advances. After the end of the Freedmen's Bureau efforts in

---

[178] The failure to resolve them were later actively reflected in Fergusson and St. Louis protests.

[179] *Records of the Field Office for the State of Missouri, Bureau of Refugees, Freedmen, and Abandoned Lands* (Freedmen's Bureau) for Missouri, 1865–1872."

[180] Ibid.

Missouri it became clear that any other assistance would have to come from Missouri citizens and the state government. Governor Fletcher led the efforts but there were many others who accepted responsibility for these tasks. They all met with resistance.

While the Freedmen's Bureau had assisted with the establishment of black schools in St. Louis, Warrensburg, Kansas City, Westport, and Carondelet, education outside of the large metropolitan areas remained almost non-existent for former slaves. It also was inadequate for white children. There were some groups that did help as possible. But the first black high school, Sumner, in St. Louis, did not open until 1875.[181] Even so, before the end of Fletcher's term benevolent societies like the American Missionary Society and the Western Freedmen's Aid Society had created over thirty elementary schools for black children in Missouri. They were especially assisted by the generosity of the German community.[182] The governor gave vocal and personal support to all of these efforts. His words could and did generate dollars for the worthy causes.

Regardless of Fletcher's efforts, public education made little advance in outstate Missouri for any children or young people of any race during the fifty years after the Civil War. However, one attempt to help black children stood out above all others. Fletcher had supported the active creation of many educational institutions for black children and he got his chance to publicly demonstrate his commitment as the result of a remarkable chain of events.

During the war, the 61st and 65th Missouri Regiments of Colored Infantry had been posted to Benton Barracks in north St. Louis.[183] These regiments included former free-blacks and former slaves. Most were at least functionally illiterate. The military command both encouraged and required the soldiers to gain literacy. The Federal military command believed an educated soldier would be a better soldier. Reading, Writing and Arithmetic became as important as musket loading, close-order drill, and rifle practice at Benton Barracks. Slowly, the efforts worked with the eager black recruits. They thirsted for the knowledge that they had been denied.

---

[181] *Walk in St. Louis,* Missouri Historical Society, n.d.

[182] Records of the Field Office.

[183] Today it is called Fairground Park in St. Louis; located at Grand and Natural Bridge.

At the end of the war these same soldiers, truly appreciating their education, decided to "give back" to others. They helped create Lincoln Institute (later Lincoln University) in Jefferson City, Missouri. Each payday during the last year or so of the war and as long as they wore the blue uniform, a donation would be made by each soldier. Eventually over five thousand dollars (equal to *about seventy-five thousand dollars in 2018*) were raised, a sight chosen and a board of trustees created. Governor

Statue dedicated to African-American Infantry located at Lincoln University, Jefferson City, Missouri; Public Domain.

Thomas C. Fletcher served as the first President of the Trustees. J. A. Yeatman, founder of Mercantile Library in St. Louis, served as treasurer. Fletcher and his fellow trustees presented the Articles of Incorporation to Cole County Circuit Court on June 25, 1866. As with NIMBY (*not in my back yard*) in modern America, resistance rapidly began to emerge across the state. The opposition lamented the fact that this school was for blacks when white children also needed schools. Fletcher and his fellow trustees had to deal with the resistance. They came up with a course of action that would mute the opposition. A few months after the vocal opposition began, Fletcher presented a Lincoln Institute Constitution that explained that while the purpose of the institution primarily focused on black children, the doors would also be open to others.[184] This explanation effectively thwarted many opposed to helping black children while white children still needed assistance. In effect it said to white parents that their children could come to the black school—not a likely prospect. But this provided political "cover" for the effort. The governor had learned how to deal the political

---

[184] Lincoln University has continued that tradition and is a fully integrated institution today.

realities in both the legislature and in the public opinion arenas. While governor, Fletcher continued to serve as a Trustee and successfully lobbied for the State support which guaranteed the future success of the school. While he lived in the governor's mansion he also led the efforts to secure additional private funds for the school from the state citizenry.[185] Clara likely worked with him to accomplish the task; the mission fit with her own philosophy and dedication.

This success, notwithstanding, African-Americans after the war continued to endure great limitations; none of which Fletcher would be able to change. He did, however, support the freed slaves and black community as possible. He had enrolled many African-Americans in the State Militia where they played a significant role in overseeing elections, removing recalcitrant officer holders, and patrolling the counties.[186] They served with distinction. This gained Fletcher much notoriety from organizations like the notorious Knights of the Golden Circle and its supporting newspaper The Weekly Caucasian. As late as 1868 this Missouri newspaper noted that, "*Ten states in the Union have been territoralized (sic) and africanized (sic) by these....and 4,000,000 ignorant barbarians have been made superior to 10,000,000 of white men...there is danger ahead.*"[187] Danger, indeed, did rear up. Across Missouri, black schools and churches were burned, teachers were intimidated and many whites voiced opposition to any black advancement. The Democratic Party voiced opposition to most legislative changes although the Radicals retained control—for the most part. The Radicals tried unsuccessfully to get the state to give the vote to black males. Racism still had significant influence if not actual power in both parties.

The governor also actively supported the efforts to gain the franchise for black males from the national congress. As President Johnson revealed his anti-black sentiments, opposition to him began to surface. Fletcher became a national leader in the opposition to the racially-biased U. S. President. During the summer and fall of 1865 Fletcher crossed the state

---

[185] Lincoln University Archives, "The Founding of Lincoln University," 4-6.; Lincoln Institute: Articles of Incorporation.

[186] *The Howard Union,* November 23, 1865, 1.

[187] *The Weekly Caucasian_*(Lexington, Missouri), February 22, 1868, 2.

lobbying for his doctrine of *"equal rights and reconciliation"* in Missouri.[188] He gave the principle address to the Equal Rights League in St. Louis and then went further.[189] In 1866, he presided over a Southern Unionists and Loyalists Convention in the National Union Clubhouse, Philadelphia, Pennsylvania. This group voiced loud concerns about Johnson's pro-Southern views and the past and continuing Southern religious support for slavery.[190] Hundreds of newspapers reported the efforts of Fletcher and others in regard to the possible impeachment of the sitting president.

Newspaper Banner, 1866; Public Domain.

Everyone did not support his efforts on behalf of African-Americans. One unexpected opponent, Frank Blair, had moved toward a more racist perspective and opposed Radical Republican support for freed slaves or any blacks in general. The tension between Fletcher and his mentor, Frank Blair, resulted in great pain—probably for them both. Regardless of any and all opposition, the governor began to gain national attention and great respect. He became seen as a voice of moderate determination in a sea of radicalism.[191]

---

188   Parish, *Missouri Under Radical Rule*, 133.

189   Ibid. 136.

190   *The Daily Journal* (Wilmington, North Carolina), September 6, 1866, 2; *Richmond Dispatch*, September 4, 1866, 3.

191   Regardless of Blair's opposition, Fletcher continued to respect him and even in later life told any listeners who were interested how great a man Blair had been.

Fletcher Tackles the Economy

F letcher knew that no one, white or black, would succeed and prosper without security and economic stability; racial inequality notwithstanding. He knew that recovery required money and people. The Civil War had already caused hundreds of thousands of people to leave Missouri over the four years after Fort Sumter had been fired upon. The state needs, Fletcher told the people, *"all the inhabitants she can get." don't run off the returning rebels."*[192] That was just the beginning of his efforts to deal with the problems of limited labor. In early 1869 he announced that the state had lost over four hundred thousand inhabitants in just the last year.[193] Some estimates assert the state had lost nearly one third of the pre-war population by 1868.[194] How to replace these and substantially increase the total population became a significant question across the state and certainly in Jefferson City. The return of Missourians who had joined rebel forces assisted in expanding the labor force but came home with their own set of problems. Fletcher, time and again noted their general positive impact on the state and continually urged others to be glad they were home and helping the state recover from the devastation of the war. He had fewer positive things to say about pro-South Missourians

---

[192] *The Howard Union*, July 20, 1865, 3.

[193] *Nashville Union and American,* ibid.

[194] Parish, *Missouri Under Radical Rule*, 178.

who had supported guerillas and general insurrection. Neither did he have any toleration for pro-Union Missourians who had not participated in the military but seemed to take great pleasure in causing problems for others. The governor over and over berated them for their negativity and antagonism toward the returning rebels and their supporters. He felt that their efforts worked against the increase of population the state needed. Perhaps, Lincoln's concept of reconciliation still resonated with him.

Fletcher and his supporters looked eastward in the United States and across the Atlantic to western Europe for new immigration. The governor believed only a *"Herculean"* effort would be successful. The State's lawmakers needed to enact laws and create an effective bureaucracy that would be needed to facilitate the recruitment of thousands of immigrants to Missouri. They needed a special commission or board to develop and lead the crusade. He lobbied the state legislators to create this in their next session. They listened. The Missouri legislature approved Fletcher's request to create a State Board of Immigration in February, 1865.[195] Fletcher supported Isidor Bush to be its Secretary. Bush had fled Europe in 1849 and published the first Jewish weekly newspaper in New York. He had served in the U.S. Treasury Department, developed wine-grapes near Fletcher's home in Jefferson County, Missouri, served as an aide to John Charles Fremont, worked on the Iron Mountain Railroad with Fletcher and had been a member of the Missouri State Constitution Convention.[196] Under Bush's leadership, this new board then asked counties to create emigrant societies to welcome new arrivals and encouraged them to reach out across the country themselves.[197] The board members also began their own efforts to create a professional campaign to encourage migration to Missouri.

Fletcher did not just support the establishment of this board and then let them do everything. Intermittently over the next several years he traveled across Missouri and then made many trips to Eastern cities to advertise the advantages of his beloved state. In one of the first such trips,

[195] Ibid. 181.

[196] "Isidor Bush, Jewish Pioneer, A Man for All Seasons, St. Louis, Missouri," *www. JMAW.org.*

[197] *Holt County Sentinel,* (Oregon, Missouri) April 5, 1867, 2.

made only six months after the Board organized, he spoke in St. Joseph. In addition to complimenting them on their initial efforts, he made comments he would repeat again and again over the next few years in Missouri and eastern states. He touted "... *the peculiarities and capabilities of our soil, the varieties and localities of our mineral, the extent and qualities of our timber, the number and availability of our water courses, the nature and adaptability of our climate, the facilities for railway and other communication and transportation, the opportunities for education, the evidences of complete tranquility, and other subjects of interest to those removal form an old to a new country.*"[198] The "*complete tranquility*" may have been a bit exaggerated, but much had improved across Missouri. Fletcher also reiterated "*the great need of our State is more people*" and noted of the immigrants coming to Missouri that "*the class of people finding homes among us comprises men of intelligence, native energy and industrious habits, such as are calculated to augment our wealth and support and strengthen all the best interests of a State.*"[199]

In regard to Fletcher's home county, Jefferson, an out-state newspaper announced in 1867 that, "*The Jefferson County Emigration Society is doing a good work for that county. According to the* Leader *three thousand pamphlets in English, and three thousand maps of Jefferson county, have now been printed by the society, for general distribution, and a German edition is completed. Scarcely in any better than this can the counties of our State promote their material interests.*"[200] The city of Warrenton sought woolen mills and told prospective immigrants, "*Come on with your machinery and we will give you a good welcome, and in ten years if you don't get rich it will be your own fault.*"[201] Over eleven-thousand miles of rivers and extensive lake systems promised water for agriculture. Wine-grapes thrived across the low-hillsides. Cattle found abundant grasslands and adequate water. The famous Missouri Mule provided efficient and dependable field labor.

Fletcher's and the Board's extensive efforts quickly began to be successful. *The Holt County Sentinel* soon reported that "*thousands [from*

---

[198] *Holt County Sentinel*, November 17, 1865, p.1.

[199] Ibid.

[200] *Holt County Sentinel*, April 19, 1867, 2.

[201] *Warrenton Banner* (Warrenton, Missouri), June 29, 1869, 2.

Europe] are emigrating thence directly for Missouri."[202] In 1867 The Macon Argus reported that "... (in Sedalia) *Within the last ninety days we estimate that 6,750 wagons have passed through the city—on an average, seventy-five per day. These wagons nearly all contained families averaging five in number. The aggregate number, then, passed though is 33,750.... It affords us much pleasure to know that nearly all these immigrants were induced to come to Missouri on account of her loyal government."*[203]

Kansas City and St. Louis both greatly benefited from Fletcher's and the Board's efforts. Commerce increased and sales to immigrants boosted the local economies. The regions across the state touted their respective value to the potential newcomers with glowing accounts of the fertile soil, abundant water resources, available transportation, mild climate, copious stands of timber, strong health of its citizens, remunerative employment, just and equitable laws and political stability among other attributes. In the year after Fletcher left office, the census noted that Missouri had increased from the eighth most populous state to the fifth.[204] Some of these were former Confederates or families whose livelihood had been trampled by military operations in southern and/or border states. Others had fled the eastern cities where industrialization displaced them or devalued their labor. Missouri offered a ray of sunshine in an otherwise cloudy future for many young ambitious individuals and families across the nation.

Even with available land, effective farming techniques and adequate numbers of industrious people, goods had to be transported to market. When Fletcher took office, this could not easily happen. At the beginning of 1865, only one railroad worked at least semi-regularly. It only ran between St. Louis and Kansas City. Thousands of miles which had been planned, lay on engineers' drawing tables or in ruins. Fletcher's administration took a bold and controversial tact. Most of the railroads in the state had been underwritten by the State with liens—essentially first mortgages. Every railroad in Missouri defaulted by the end of

---

[202] *Holt County Sentinel,* November 17, 1865, 2.

[203] *Macon Argus* (Macon, Missouri), December 25, 1867, 1.

[204] Duane G. Meyer, *The Heritage of Missouri,* River City Publishers (St. Louis, Missouri), 1988. 437-438.

1860.[205] During the war operating or trying to build a rail line proved very dangerous as guerillas burned bridges, blew up rolling stock and shot workers.

Governor Fletcher quickly used his power and increasing influence with the legislature to foreclose on all the railroads. He then took them over for the state. His goals in doing so included incentivizing local support, stabilizing the railroad companies, rapidly building the needed lines, revitalizing the state's rail infrastructure and then equably disposing of the state's financial interests as soon as practicable. He established a task force that actually operated one railroad and supervised all the others.[206] Thereafter, counties needing transportation often passed bond issues to support the proposed rail construction. Lafayette, a county particularly torn by strife, supported the effort at a meeting where over two hundred people "almost unanimously" support the effort.[207] These actions drew national attention. On June 21, 1867, an eastern newspaper announced,

> *Governor Fletcher today took possession of the Atlantic and Pacific railroad, formerly known as the Northeast Branch of the Missouri Pacific, which was purchased from the State by General Fremont and his associates, the purchaser having neglected to pay the first annual installment, due June 15, and otherwise failed to perform their contract. The road has been placed in charge of General C.B. Fisk, of St. Louis. The Governor's action meets the hearty approval of the people of Southwest Missouri, and the citizens of Rolla held a mass meeting, at which Governor Fletcher spoke.[208]*

All of Fletcher's efforts did not, however, appease or please everyone. The seizure of railroads, operation and then disposal resulted in major controversies. The consistently anti-Fletcher newspaper, The *Weekly*

---

[205] Parish, *Missouri Under Radical Rule*, 193.

[206] *St. Louis Post-Dispatch*, December 29, 1907, 11.

[207] *The Weekly Caucasian*, February 22, 1868, 2.

[208] *Harrisburg Telegraph*, June 22, 1867, 1.

Caucasian, called the governor, *"Seizure the Great."*[209] *"Bribery"* and *"corruption"* were yelled at the state capital but an investigation cleared the Fletcher administration from any wrongdoing.[210] The state never did have all its investments returned nor did they expect to. Their efforts focused on developing the crucial transportation lines for the state. Under Fletcher's bold action, railroad lines were completed and commerce restored in a relatively short period of time—less than three years. This meant that the state's economy could rapidly grow and compete with other agricultural centers in the United States. This early infrastructure investment worked in Missouri. Public money generated private investment and provided economic stimulus for almost all industrial and capitalistic ventures. Agricultural markets expanded from *"nearby"* to hundreds of miles from the farm. St. Louis beer could be shipped to New Orleans or Austin. Business transactions that often took a week of travel could be accomplished in a few days or so. The governor had a clear understanding of the need for a stable and extensive railroad system to grow the economy. His past role as legal counsel and land developer for the Iron Mountain railroad before the war probably helped develop and hone his perspective. Fletcher's actions toward the railroads set the stage for future growth; and did not hurt his own career prospects either. The railroad industry paid close attention to his positive actions that helped their development and expansion.

Another issue mentioned in his inaugural address, education, became a major part of the first legislative session. Although many supported the concept, or at least said they did, education really did not receive much attention until 1866. The legislature, with prodding from Governor Fletcher and others, passed a new School Law. It provided for the creation of a school district in each Missouri Congressional Township and allowed local sub-districts as needed. Three males were elected in each Township who would manage and control the schools, employee teachers, and certify the salaries for payment. Township Boards of Education were also created. They would determine the rules and regulations for local

---

[209] *The Weekly Caucasian,* February 8, 1868, 1.
[210] Parish, *Missouri Under Radical Rule,* 201-202.

governance, determine the studies and books to be used and establish elementary and secondary schools. The Boards also had to deal with the issue of schools for *"colored students."* This may have been added, at least to some extent, due to the efforts of Tom Fletcher who adamantly supported the extension of education to black Americans. Boards were required to *"...provide separate schools when the whole number of (black) enumeration exceeds twenty, so as to afford them the advantage and privileges of a common school education; in case the number of colored students should be less than twelve for any one month, it shall be the duty of the Board to discontinue such school."*[211] A superintendent also would be created in each county. This man, who had to be a qualified teacher, would serve for two years and could be reelected. He would hire teachers that had a *"...valid certification, good moral character and could teach orthography, reading in English, penmanship, arithmetic, English grammar, modern geography, and the history of the United States."*[212] Fletcher wanted someone to head this effort who was in alignment with his own goals and attitudes. He turned to a friend and fellow Radical Republican.

Thomas A. Parker became the first State School Superintendent. Advising him in matters related to black Americans' education was James Milton Turner. Turner had served as a body servant to Governor Fletcher's brother in law, Madison Miller, during the Civil War. But, his work with the Freedman's Bureau had brought him to the attention of the governor in a more professional manner. Turner, as a child, had been sold on the St. Louis Court House steps and then later purchased by his father. He became aide to Madison Miller in the first part of the war and later became active in the Radical Republican Party's efforts for Ulysses Grant and worked in the Freedman's Bureau. Later, when Turner successfully sought a federal appointment as Minister to Liberia, Fletcher supported his choice by the Federal Government. He wrote to President Grant explaining that described Turner as an, *"...intelligent and energetic young man and a true patriot.... I have personal knowledge of his integrity*

---

[211] *Holt County Sentinel,* May 4, 1866, 2.
[212] Ibid.

as a man and think him eminently an upright man."[213] Five years later, with no sense of irony, one newspaper described Turner as *"...a genuine negro, but one of the finest specimens of the race we ever saw... educated, well informed on the on the political topics of the day is a first class orator...."*[214] Under Parker and, to some extent, Turner, Missouri schools did expand and do so quickly. For several years early in this term, Parker traversed the state meeting with Townships and teachers to stimulate the growth in education. In early 1868 Missouri school data illustrated the success. The number of teachers increased from less than one thousand in 1865 to 6,262 in January of 1868. Over one thousand five hundred school houses were built just in 1867 bringing the total in the state to 4,840. Even the school libraries expanded. In March, 1868 the state report noted there were 15,644 books in schools across the state. And, 476,192 children between the ages of five to twenty were enrolled in schools; of which 32,494 were African-American.[215] Parker and Turner constantly faced racism that complicated and confounded many of their respective efforts to bring education to the black communities in Missouri. Their results were mixed.

Of course, other, less dramatic issues also drew the young governor's attention during his term. One such instance involved his appointment of Charles Valentine Riley as Missouri's State Entomologist—only the third such appointment in the United States. Later, this scientist provided the answer to France's aphid devastation by using Missouri plants to replace French infected ones. This saved wine-making in France. He also saved Missouri crops from locust infestations and brought agriculture science to Missouri farm families.

Fletcher also assisted in other areas of need. He calmed and assisted the cattle breeders of the state when passing Texas cattle infected local animals. He supported a state mandate that required "wintering over" (i.e. quarantining) foreign cattle for a period.[216] Fletcher led the successful

---

[213] Gary R. Kremer, *James Milton Turner and the Promise of America,* Columbia, University of Missouri Press, 1991. 43.

[214] *The Lincoln County Herald,* November 3, 1870, 2,

[215] *Weekly Caucasian,* January 18, 1868, 1; *Macon Argus,* March 4, 1868, 1.

[216] *The Courier-Journal* (Louisville, Kentucky), September 24, 1866, 1.

effort to bridge the Missouri River at St Charles. He led the efforts to create an "Soldiers' Home" for veterans in need of medical and old age care. The national Republican governors' vocal opposition to President Johnson was initiated by Fletcher.[217] The notorious quote from Johnson, *"This is a country for white men, and by God, as long as I am president, it shall be a government for white men"* had been made to Fletcher as the representative of the governors and reported as such by the *Cincinnati Enquirer*.[218] He also became a well-known and well-respected figure in Washington D.C. during his term of office.

His wife, Clara, continued to be his greatest supporter and one of his great assets. She maintained the Governor's Mansion and took care of others in Jefferson City in many ways. In 1867, the wife of Colonel W. A. Grosman, a close friend of hers and the governor, contracted typhoid fever and needed care. They had no family nearby and Clara stepped in. Clara nursed her in the governor's mansion for several weeks until she died.[219] Clara could be counted on to be there for their friends and for her own children throughout his term of office. Governor Fletcher frequently had to be absent for governmental responsibilities. Clara held down the home front while he traveled or otherwise occupied himself. And, he had much to do and very little time in which to accomplish his goals. Governors in Missouri could only have one term of office.

By the end of his one term, the state had restored, for the most part, its civil safety. Free and fair elections had been guaranteed, sometimes supported by the bayonet. The judicial system worked; for the most part. The State war debt had been significantly reduced. The public-school system had greatly improved although still remained inadequate. The population had increased by almost fifty percent and Missouri had increased from being ranked as the seventh largest state for agricultural productivity to fifth in the nation.[220] The entire state rail system functioned or bordered on functioning well. Even river traffic had been mostly restored although still declined due to the increase in

---

[217] *The Plymouth Democrat* (Plymouth, Indiana)., September 12, 1867, 2.

[218] Hans Louis Trefousse, *Andrew Johnson*, W.W. Norton & Company, 1997, 236.

[219] *Atchison Daily Champion* (Atchison, Kansas), March 22, 1867, 3.

[220] Parish, *Missouri Under Radical Rule*, 185-186.

railroad competition. African-Americans were free. Many could attend elementary schools, especially if they lived in St. Louis. The vote still eluded black males but all knew it would be provided very soon as the Thirteenth Amendment had the support of the Missouri Legislature. Racism, however, did not cease, but a dent had been made in it. The Radical Republicans had control of the legislature, the courts, most of the legal system and voting registration. People across the state could breathe easier and not fear to take a trip from one city or farm to another. While *"normalcy"* did not totally exist, it surely stood just a short distance away after Fletcher's term of office. The light at the end of the tunnel would not prove to be a train; a significant improvement in just four years.

As the 1868 election neared Fletcher likely did not lament the fact that the state constitution prevented him from a second term. His name came up as a potential choice to be Grant's Vice President, a minister to Berlin, or for some other national position.[221] Fletcher did not encourage this, although his friendship with Ulysses Grant continued and he assisted the formal commander in his effort to obtain the presidency. He made many trips across the state to insure the support from Missouri for his old friend. He also had meetings with Grant to discuss the upcoming election and strategy needed in the west. Grant paid close attention to the advice Tom gave him. Part of this mutual trust came from Fletcher's wartime experience serving under Grant and Sherman. The bond of battle had developed confidence. Likely, the trust bestowed on Fletcher by Abraham Lincoln also endeared him to Grant. Others in Washington D.C. and in the East noted the influence the soon-to-be ex-governor had with soon-to-be president, Ulysses Grant. Even a Southern newspaper, the *Richmond Dispatch,* took notice when Grant and Fletcher had a meeting in late 1867.[222] The governor's position of respect and influence on the national level had become obvious. Many across the nation and across Missouri looked at Fletcher as a consistent, brilliant and just person; even if they did not always agree with him.

His personal honesty and reputation also encouraged support from

---

[221] *The Weekly Caucasian* (Lexington, Missouri), May 23, 1868, 1.
[222] *Richmond Dispatch,* October 1, 1867, 3.

unlikely groups. The Missouri Democratic Party approached him to lead their ticket by running for the U. S. Senate as a Democrat. They recognized him as a moderate person of integrity and ability that did not blindly follow the Radical wing of the Republican Party. They probably noted his actions in December, 1867, when a large controversy occurred over the special election in the Third District. Despite all attempts to secure the seat for a Republican, Fletcher certified the contested results for the Democrat.[223] While somewhat interested in the 1868 campaign for the Senate he would not accept Democratic support. When approached by the Missouri Democrats who looked at him as being separate from the Radical Republicans they hated, he responded, *"Gentlemen, I am a Republican. I differ with you in politics and do not desire your support; if I am elected to the United States Senate I will go in elected by Republican members of the Missouri legislature, or I will stay home."*[224] He stayed home— Drake had the election locked up and the railroad controversies complicated Fletcher's reluctant contemplation of the contest for the senate seat.[225]

[223] *Arkansas Gazette* (Little Rock, Arkansas), December 14, 1867, 2.

[224] *Fort Scott Weekly Monitor* (Fort Scott, Kansas), August 19, 1868, 4.

[225] *Hartford Courant* (Hartford, Connecticut), November 16, 1866, 4.

Private Citizen, the Early Days

S erving as the governor of Missouri had been rewarding in many ways but, personally, it been a financial blow to Tom Fletcher. His state salary covered many of his expenses but not nearly all. Fortunately for him and for his family, Fletcher had been successful in land dealings in and around De Soto before becoming governor. During his term of office, he had sold a large number of his assets to supplement his meager income as governor. Not an extremely wealthy person, at the end of his term Fletcher needed to generate a sufficient income to support his family. Governmental positions, even on the federal level did not offer enough income to establish residences in both Missouri and Washington D. C. He decided to return to St. Louis and practice law but keep his options open. His extremely positive contacts with railroad companies over his term as governor also probably assured his employment as a counsel for railroads. His future looked bright.

In addition to his own financial issues, once out of the political arena he needed to look at what he really wanted to do with the rest of his life in other meaningful ways. He turned forty-two years of age just after leaving office; still a young man. Obviously, his family had to be a center-point of his life. Clara and he spend many hours thinking about the options available to them. Their families in De Soto certainly would have loved for them to return to Jefferson County and live out their lives there. While attractive in some ways, Tom's life experiences had forever changed him. He would never be content as a small town and even regionally focused attorney. There were now other areas of importance. Clara found St. Louis to be much more appealing than living a rural life.

Tom's military experiences had changed his life and still influenced him. He could not look to the future without seeing himself being involved with veterans' affairs in some way or another. The Republican Party had given him his career, but also caused great strife. Still, he looked toward some significant involvement with the party and the party base centered in St. Louis. Obviously, the city would be the first place he and Clara would consider living. The children would have access to a good education and the family would live around people who shared their views. Clara had interests in the arts, education, and the growth of St. Louis. She loved the city's cosmopolitan nature—at least she perceived it so. Tom especially felt drawn to music and art. He soon served as the treasurer of the effort to establish an opera house in St. Louis, the forerunner of Powell Hall.[226] He likely also kept at least one eye on potential public service and potential positions in government that might fit his life and career goals. He also enjoyed being considered for them. His legal practice would not be hurt by his name being frequently mentioned in papers across the nation as being under consideration for one Federal position or another.

Although living in the mid-west, Fletcher also kept his eye very closely focused on the national capital. He had established a significantly positive reputation with national leaders including senators, representatives, and department staff during his term as governor. He believed that these contacts in Washington D. C., including especially the new president, Ulysses S. Grant, would enhance his influence. Fletcher further believed that his friendship with St. Louis city leaders, former and current military leaders like Wm T. Sherman and Fletcher's intimate knowledge of federal and state government would also enhance his attractiveness to potential clients. Even his membership in the Knights Templar, a Freemason organization would cultivate his important contacts. His thoughts proved correct although he never became an extremely wealthy person.

---

[226] *St. Louis Post Dispatch,* May 4, 1874, 4.

Tom Fletcher initially opened his St. Louis law practice in an office at 212 north 3rd Street and later moved to the Second National Bank Building; a more visible location. He moved his family into a new home at No. 3 Minnesota Avenue in the mostly undeveloped South St. Louis.[227] Working in St. Louis, Jefferson City and Washington D. C., he knew that he would have to travel much but still felt young and energetic. In his early forties, Fletcher enthusiastically looked forward to a long and successful career. He didn't forget his roots either. He found time to file the incorporations for the new city of De Soto shortly after leaving the governor's office and then donated land for the creation of a Catholic church to serve many of the men working on the railroad and their families living in the *Fountain City*.[228]

As a well-known personality, Fletcher drew clients with a variety of legal problems. In the early months of his burgeoning career, he accepted most requests. He needed the money. But, soon he found that his influence in the political halls and state legislative and judicial realms could be very important to others in addition to and, perhaps more, than his legal expertise that was considerable. In Jefferson City and St. Louis, he soon brought cases to the Federal District Court and intervened with state agencies and the state legislature in more political rather than legal matters. With his contacts in Washington D.C., Missourians and others sought his assistance when there were issues with federal departments, especially related to railroads, mining, Native-American, African-American or other western issues. His extensive and expert legal abilities eventually led him to frequently practice before the United States Supreme Court.[229]

He became very visible in the state and national capitals. A *"person of importance,"* Fletcher's comings and goings became of interest to many across the nation. Even when he just checked into one of the Washington D.C. hotels his doing so warranted at least a mention on page two or three of many eastern papers. Attending a party with Missouri legislators could

---

[227] *1870 Gould's City Directory,* Missouri Historical Society, St. Louis, Missouri 76; 86.

[228] De Soto Historical Society, *De Soto Missouri: A Pictorial History,* self-published, no date.

[229] *St. Louis Post-Dispatch,* February 21, 1899, 8.

merit the front page. His family also received attention just because they were associated with him. In December, 1870, the death of Clement B. Fletcher, his father, received a short paragraph in *The Titusville Herald* of Pennsylvania even though Clement had never been near Titusville.[230] He was, however, Thomas Fletcher's father and thus of interest to those interested in Tom. And many were. In 1871 *The Chicago Tribune* noted that *"John Brill, a servant at the executive mansion during Governor Fletcher's term, was kicked by a horse and killed, last Saturday."*[231] Tom's influence continued to grow; he had many friends in government. His name became familiar to many, if not most Americans.

One of Fletcher's friends, President Grant, had been a capable general but proved to be less so as head-of-state. There were few "Fletchers" in his cabinet. Mostly mediocre, some appointees were actually incredibly unscrupulous. Even Grant's brother-in-law became involved with financial practices of questionable legality. The *Credit Mobilier*, a fraudulent railroad construction company became the national symbol of corruption as it bribed legislators, and even compromised the Vice President, Schuyer Colfax. Others would follow in a myriad of schemes to defraud the nation. While never personally involved with these horrendous schemes, Grant felt the disappointment and embarrassment resultant from the involvement of his friends. Under his ineffective leadership, the national leadership began to move toward thirty years or so of *"the best government money could buy;"* with emphasis on the word *"buy"* or maybe a better word would be *"bribe."* In spite of these calamities, for the eight years of his term, Grant attempted to execute the laws, promote sound money, and follow a humane policy toward the Native-Americans.

In regard to the Native-Americans, Grant adopted a new approach: a so called *"Peace Policy."* This well-meaning effort brought a philanthropic commission on board, replaced the Interior Department's agents with army officers and created mostly self-governing Native-American reservations.[232] Although having some very limited success in the reservation system, he failed in most other efforts. He remained loyal

---

[230] *The Titusville Herald* (Titusville, Pennsylvania), December 1, 1870, 2.

[231] *Chicago Tribune* (Chicago, Illinois), December 14, 1871, 2.

[232] H.W. Brands, *Man Who Saved the Nation*, 564.

to his subordinates—at least until they were in jail. Fletcher, however, remained his friend throughout the years. Their common military bond held them together. And, while Fletcher would use his influence with the president from time to time, he never violated the president's trust. This allowed him access. Access to political figures can be perceived as power. And businesses and corporations that operated across state lines needed access to legislators.

In 1872, The Pacific Railroad reorganized into the Missouri Pacific Railroad; Fletcher remained a principle legal counselor for the line. As such, he warranted a railroad pass that ensured him free travel on any line (*a practice continued by most railroads well until the early 1960's for VIPs and engineers with their spouses and immediate family members*). While the Panic of 1873 slowed the railroad expansion, it did not stop it. Fletcher continued to arrange land purchases and secure "right-of-way's" as part of his general duties. His experiences as governor gave him the knowledge and governmental contacts to facilitate such purchases and to facilitate mutual agreements between lines with federal approval. He became well known and respected by the railroad industry across the nation; especially in Washington. D. C.

Throughout his post-gubernatorial career, Fletcher became involved with important and often controversial issues. His work took him

back and forth between St. Louis and Washington, D.C. where he would stay at the Ebbitt House or Harris House, both very prestigious locations in the city.[233] Clara would accompany him on some but not all trips. The demands from Washington increased as his successes continued to grow.

Ebbits House Hotel in Washington D. C. where Fletcher often stayed; Public Domain.

---

[233] Newspapers frequently alerted the readers of the presence of this important figure in Washington, D. C. when he stayed at one of these locations.

Fletcher and the Native-Americans

Oe issue became more of an adventure than a business dealing to the former governor. In 1875 Fletcher interrupted his law practice to assist a friend, President Grant. Fletcher agreed to head an investigation regarding the Red Cloud reservation. Regardless of the negative views of many historians towards the president, Grant really wanted fair treatment for Native-Americans. He frequently turned to some favorite westerners like Robert Campbell and Thomas Fletcher for advice. He knew that Fletcher had experience in working with Native-Americans. The ex-governor had successfully negotiated a treaty *"with the "Shownees (sic) and Wyandotte Indians for the right of way for a railroad through their respective reservations."* The Wyandottes were experienced in dealing with the white government and, although their numbers had been significantly reduced, they still held important land for railroad expansion in Kansas. The treaty negotiated by Fletcher gave the railroad *"unobstructed right of way from the western border of Missouri to the Colorado River."*[234] The agreement worked for both sides in this instance—due to the negotiation capabilities of the Native-Americans and of Thomas Fletcher. Washington D. C. bureaucrats took notice of

---

[234] *Baltimore Sun* (Baltimore, Maryland), February 14, 1871, 1.

this success. And, Grant trusted his old friend. That couldn't be said of many of the president's acquaintances.

Grant oversaw a powder-keg in the lands between Kansas and California. A major national and ethical problem existed in regard to the native peoples who lived there. Broken down to the basics, the issue seemed to be, "*What can and should we* (the dominant Eurocentric culture) *do about these people?*" There were competing realities. On the Great Plains the life of the indigenous peoples involved mobility and sacred spaces. They followed the buffalo. This majestic animal provided them food, shelter, utensils, and basically, their life. They looked at sacred spaces such as the Black Hills as gifts from the Great Spirit and assumed stewardship for them. To the Eurocentric spreading population, the Indians were in the way and needed to be removed. Some advocated placing them on reservations as had been done with those Native-Americans who had lived east of the Mississippi. Others were okay with extermination. Some wanted assimilation with the dominant culture to be the final result. While the reservations were limitedly successful in Oklahoma with Native-Americans who had never followed the buffalo, the reservations in the Great Plains were mostly abysmal failures— still are.

Fletcher, like all Americans, knew that the treatment of the indigenous people on reservations had become a national controversy. Racism competed with paternalism for control of the reservations. In order to provide the best supervision, the government had, with the best of intentions, appointed various religious groups to oversee reservations. Quakers took over almost half of them. The myopic religious power-structures attempted to destroy what was integral to the Native-Americans—their paradigms of life, spirituality and culture. They started with the children and attempted to rid them of their barbarian dress, hair styles, language and ethnicity. But, they also challenged the entire culture's mobile and naturally integrative way of life. Replacing this with dependency upon mostly inadequate Federal treaties effectively created hostility that has lasted to the modern era. Personal and tribal pride, an essential part of the Native-American life, ended with the reservation system. Hunger also became part of the daily attempt to exist when treaties were not honored by the white establishment. Rampant and prolific alcohol consumption, for which indigenous peoples had no natural tolerance levels, sped the decline.

Opportunistic sutlers of questionable ability and/or honesty were entrusted by the government with the provision of all supplies desperately needed by the reservation-bound tribes. They arranged for the delivery of flour, meat, blankets, sugar, medicine and other basic needs. Winter blankets arrived on the Montana reservation that could almost be seen through. Thousand-pound cows were billed to the government at the rate for a fifteen-hundred one. Flour arrived with sawdust in it or infested with weevils. Even just general every-day supplies seldom arrived in sufficient quantities for the dependent tribal members. The sutlers positions themselves were frequently sold or traded for political purposes or cash by the notorious national "Indian Ring."[235] President Grant's Secretary of War, William Worth Belknap, had created a financial bonanza for himself and other nefarious friends. These corrupt governmental bureaucrats took bribes, provided sub-standard goods or none at all as they pocketed vast amounts of money. Eventually, in 1876 Belknap faced impeachment by the Senate but left the government without conviction.

In May, just before Fletcher's investigation began in 1875, fellow St. Louisian, Robert Campbell, and four other federal Commissioners of Indian Affairs had resigned *en masse* in disgust with the federal system.[236] Rumors of incompetency, fraud, and maltreatment at the agencies pervaded the national news. The latest issue focused on the Red Cloud Agency. The criticism had been brought to national attention by a young paleontologist who had been working nearby. He became appalled at what he perceived as a horrible situation on the reservation and wanted everyone to know about it. His efforts worked. Popular outrage ensued. Grant turned to Tom Fletcher and several others to look into problems at the Red Cloud Agency located at the northwest corner of Nebraska. He asked Fletcher to supervise the entire mission and write the final report. Grant wanted the truth, not a whitewash.

---

[235] Stephen F. Huss, *Take No Advantage: The Biography of Robert Campbell*, Dissertation, St. Louis University, 1989, 351.

[236] *Take No Advantage*, 353.

This difficult situation with the Sioux had not developed in a vacuum. The problem there and elsewhere related to the Sioux probably began in 1866 or so. Over two hundred hostile engagements in the Great Plains had occurred between that year and 1875; mostly with the Sioux.[237] Arapaho and Cheyenne tribes allied with the Sioux on and off, complicating the conflict for the U.S. military. The clash of cultures took the form of direct battle, treaties that were not followed by whites, and ever expanding illegal white intrusion into Native-American lands. In 1866, while negotiating a treaty in good faith with General William T. Sherman, Chief Red Cloud learned that over seven-hundred soldiers were concurrently marching toward the Powder River country. The Sioux had never agreed to allow them access to this crucial hunting ground and tribal home. The troops marched on—treaty or not. Red Cloud abruptly left the negotiations and two years of war ensued.

But, probably the events of August, 1867, really illustrated to Red Cloud the futility of continuing resistance. Thirty-two soldiers, armed with the new Henry repeating-rifle, although surrounded near Fort Kearney and vastly outnumbered, killed or wounded hundreds of Sioux warriors. Such devastating power probably demoralized Red Cloud as he withdrew to the Powder River Country (*northeastern Wyoming and southern Montana*) to contemplate the future of his tribe. By the end of 1868 a new treaty closed the trails but merely postponed further problems. Red Cloud had won the war, but in reality, had only delayed the inevitable. Under Grant, the government developed reservations created under the assumption that the native populations were "wards" rather than "nations." Native-Americans, of course, disputed this. Nevertheless, Red Cloud reluctantly led his tribe into the reservation. He had no real other choice.

In May, 1869, the Transcontinental Rail Road became a reality. Iron rails divided the Northern from the Southern Plains and destroyed the buffalo's natural migration upon which the Sioux and others depended. Massive killings of buffalo by hired white hunters that left thousands of carcasses rotting on the Plains demoralized Native Peoples. Within a

---

[237] John Tebbel, *Indian Wars*, 224

few days of the "joining of the rails," Red Cloud took a thousand Oglala Sioux to Fort Laramie to trade and collect treaty obligated provisions (annuities). They were reluctantly given the goods but told they had to move three hundred miles away to Fort Randall. Red Cloud refused.[238] An October meeting by Red Cloud with Fletcher's friend, Robert Campbell, found the chief adamant on staying near Fort Laramie.[239] Campbell could not answer Red Cloud's inquiry about the justice of white treatment in regard to his people.

By 1871 the famous chief had visited Washington D.C. and met with President Grant. He pled for justice for his people. A speaking tour drew many supporters to his cause. He returned to the reservation hopeful, but even more sure of his tribe's precarious situation. In 1873 his tribe again moved, this time to the Wind River country despite previous promises to allow them to stay where they were. Further complications arose in 1874 when the discovery of gold in the Black Hills resulted in treaty-breaking whites flooding the sacred space. Complaining to the military did no good. Whites continued their quest for gold. Violence erupted and many miners were found with arrows in them. Many young braves took the law into their own hands and then returned to the reservation after eliminating whatever whites that had appeared before their bows. Red Cloud had no control over these young warriors who came and went. They seldom participated in the formal population count needed to determine the amount of needed treaty goods promised to those living on the reservation. This inaccuracy did nothing to help assure adequate provisions and other supplies.

The situation at the new reservation became intolerable by early 1875. Professor Othniel Charles Marsh, a prominent Yale vertebrate paleontologist friendly to the Native-Americans, lodged a complaint to the Secretary of the Interior early in that year.[240] Further, he made his charges public—very public. Marsh's uncle, wealthy international

---

[238] *Take No Advantage* 347-349.

[239] Marlene Hawver, *Robert Campbell, Expectant Capitalist*, University of Nebraska, unpublished MA thesis, 98.

[240] Marsh eventually identified over five hundred new species of fossils and served on federal geological expeditions.

financier, George Peabody, had provided the funds for Marsh to pursue his vocation and kept in close communications with him. This financial independence allowed Marsh to fear no one and speak his mind as loudly as he wanted. This tie between Marsh and his powerful uncle might have encouraged the Grant administration to pay attention to the eccentric and self-convinced professor. The national news media picked up on the problems he voiced and plastered the issue in large headlines across the front pages. After discussion among military and governmental leaders, President Grant appointed ex-Governor Thomas Fletcher to head an investigation into the situation in July, 1875.[241] Also named were Hon. Benjamin W. Harris (Republican U.S. Congressman) of East Bridgewater and Charles C. Faulkner of Martinsburg, West Virginia (Democratic U.S. Congressman).

On July 22, 1875, Fletcher and members of his commission held a preliminary meeting in New York. Professor March provided each of the commissioners with a pamphlet outlining his charges. Marsh, while presenting as a bit autocratic and very self-convinced, had meticulously listed the grievances of the Sioux regarding the Red Cloud Reservation. Regardless of personal demeanor, Marsh's credentials were impeccable. The group believed the charges warranted serious attention. Fletcher and his team soon decided their next steps as they committed to a fair and unbiased investigation. The rest of the group members mostly deferred to the ex-governor. None of them had ever dealt with indigenous peoples. They also probably wanted him to deal with the professor rather than them. Each of the members left the meeting to wrap up personal issues and then proceeded to travel westward.

Only a few weeks later, in early August, Fletcher's commission arrived at Fort Laramie, Wyoming. The fort had been originally built by Robert Campbell and then later taken over by the military. It had the reputation for being secure and fairly comfortable. Experienced military used the base for patrols and provided oversight for reservations nearby. From this first stop, after a short rest from their long excursion, Fletcher and his commission members were escorted by a company of cavalry to the

---

[241] *New York Daily Herald* (New York, New York), July 15, 1875.

Red Cloud Agency located on a hill overlooking the Wind River a short distance away.

Fletcher lost no time in starting the investigation. He and the commission met first with Red Cloud and other leaders. Sitting Bull, Turkey Legs, and Man Afraid of His Horse were also in attendance. Tension permeated the meeting area. Armed soldiers stood guard at all entrances. Fletcher called the gathering to order and began the proceedings by telling the assembled group

> *We come her to see you and to talk with you, and we were selected for that purposed by the Great Father at Washington, not with the intention of making any treaties or bargains with you or of getting you to agree to anything with us, but simply to talk with you.... We were sent here to talk with you and to learn from you if any person has ill-used you in any manner. If the agent or any of the contractors who have been employed by our government to furnish you goods and supplies have cheated you we want to find that out.... The white man is very smart, you know; he will not only cheat Indians, but he will cheat white men, too, and we want you to tell us all about what has been done here.... the great body of white men want you treated right, and we are here to represent them.... We want you to be happy, want you to be rich some time or another. You must learn to raise cattle and sheep...and when you have the great herds of cattle and sheep [you] will sell them to the white man to feed the white man as the white man sends supplies to feed the Indian now.... Now, we want to talk with all of you, and we want you to tell us freely all you know about the management of affairs out here, without fear of anybody. If we can do you any good we want to do it. That is what we came for; and that is all.[242]*

---

[242] *New York Daily Herald*, August 23, 1875, 4.

Before he left for this investigation, Fletcher might have discussed the situation with his friend, Robert Campbell, who had met with Red Cloud in the past. He probably also talked with President Grant who had also met with the Indian leader and even could have had a conversation with his close friend General Wm T. Sherman who also had previously been in negotiations with Red Cloud. Fletcher took his responsibility seriously and would have used whatever resources available. In this first contact he wanted to gain the trust of the group and explain his goal—to find the truth. His introductory speech reflected his perception of Native-Americans as valued wards of the government—to whom there were serious obligations.

Red Cloud, one of the principle chiefs of the Oglala Teton Dakota (Sioux) and the leader on this reservation, rose to speak after the ex-governor sat down. A well-known warrior among the Great Plains tribes, his skills as diplomat and advocate were also admired—even by the white population. He had received great accolades on his trip eastward meeting a few months before from the politicians and then later in speaking engagements in New York City. On this trip he told the gathered whites in the audience, *"I am poor and naked, but I am the chief of the nation. We do not want riches but we do want to train our children right. Riches would do us no good. We could not take them with us to the other world. We do not want riches. We want peace and love."*[243] Newspapers divided in regard to the "Indian Question."

Red Cloud (seated second from left) and his principal tribal leaders who negotiated grievances and treaties; Public Domain.

---

[243] *www.Firstpeople.us.*

People seemed to look at the Native-Americans as "a Noble Savage" or the "Savage Animal."

Regardless of his reception, the power and sheer numbers of the white population convinced Red Cloud that it would be futile to fight any further; there could be no result other than death and genocide. Red Cloud knew that since the whites could not be defeated, he had to make the best agreements possible for his people. This meeting with Tom Fletcher and his fellow commission members provided one more opportunity to bring true understanding to the white power structure. He stood up and walked close to the former governor of Missouri seating at the end of the long room. Red Cloud's frustration seemed almost visible and he looked intently at the agency officials, commissioners and military officers. He then began his introductory remarks

> *My friends, you men that are sitting down here, do you think that you will succeed in understanding what I tell you? ...You people that are here to-day have given me this land that I am on at present.... I thought if we moved our agency up here and would come into this country we would succeed in getting more goods than we had been in the habit in getting [in our previous location]; but instead of that I succeeded backwards, and all the time I get less of everything. Last fall when the annuity goods came here...there were upwards of 300 of our people who did not get any; and everything else was short in proportion to the blankets.*[244]

He went on to explain that he believed the Great Father (president Grant) with whom he talked in the spring before this meeting but questioned those who had been responsible for purchase and delivery of the promised goods. Red Cloud explained that he knew there were somethings not under the control of the agent or the immediate subordinates. Fletcher listened closely.

---

[244] *New York Daily Herald,* Ibid.

Red Cloud wanted the commission to understand that the past experiences had not been what were promised.

> When he (an employee) must not understand the weights. When he gives rations to the old women and children he gives them out by the shovel. That does not please me…. The young men you have employed at the herds have been drunk and drinking for some time and I understand some of the cattle have been stolen and traded off…. My father (Agent Saville), we don't blame you about our provisions and goods, because you don't buy them… but you ought to see that they do well by us.
>
> There is another thing I never did like…. We didn't want soldiers here, that we didn't need them…. We don't want any army officer as an Indian agent…. We want a good man not an officer…. We don't want any man who wants to come out here to get rich. We don't want a poor man as an agent…. And I don't want a preacher as agent….[245]

In the slight pause that followed, Fletcher briefly replied, "*Professor Marsh told all these things to the Great Father… and the Great Father sent us here to see about them….*" He further promised to visit the encampments. Red Cloud then continued,

> We are all born the same—the Indians and the whites— born with five fingers on each hand; born with face and eyes and ears, and mouth to speak. There is no difference in us at all; the women are made alike, and the men are made alike, they are all about the same…. Now about those Black Hills. Our Great Father has got a great many soldiers, and I never knew him when he wanted to stop anything with his soldiers but he succeeded in it. The reason I tell you that is that the people from the States who have gone to the Black Hills are

---

[245] Ibid.

> *stealing the gold, digging it out and taking it away, and I*
> *don't see why the Great Father don't bring them back.*[246]

Acknowledging the statement, Fletcher then responded that, "*The Great Father has ordered those people to be away from there in five days from now, and if they do not go he will bring them out with soldiers.*"[247] The ex-governor probably believed that.

Famous spiritual and tactical leader, Sitting Bull, never reluctant to speak to anyone, then stood and addressed his fellow leaders, "... (talking to Old Man Afraid of His Horse) *If there is anything that Red Cloud has said that you don't like get up and speak. These gentlemen have not come here for nothing.*"[248] Sitting Bull had a long history of antagonism toward the white intrusion into the Sioux territory. Just the year before, he had defied orders to return to his assigned reservation when inadequate food supplies had been provided by the government. He had, however, reluctantly allowed Professor Marsh to hunt for fossils in the Black Hills when he finally accepted that the scholar did not seek gold. As the Commission meeting convened, Sitting Bull's formidable cavalry stood ready nearby should they be needed. The Medicine Man spoke to Fletcher not from weakness, but from a position of strength.

Fletcher, sincerely appreciating his input, if not his warriors massed outside, entreated the others, "*If there are any others who would like to speak to us we will be glad to hear them.... The white man regards Red Cloud as a great Sioux, a great warrior, a wise man.... If any have (more to say) we would like to hear from them too.*"[249]

Little Wound then stood to speak for Old Man Afraid of His Horse, explaining that the Great Father had not lived up to his promises and the agent has not accurately counted the tribal membership... among other concerns

---

[246] Ibid.

[247] Ibid.

[248] Ibid.

[249] Ibid.

[we] have not received enough for the number of Indians that have been counted.... there are a good many who are not here n ow; about one-half of them have gone out hunting... men here...are almost in distress for want of lodgings. They have to double up, two or three families in one tent, in order to get shelter. We would like to have enough tents so that each family could have a tent. The blankets we get are not good.... They told us when we moved here we were to get good clothes, such as you wear—white shirts, frock coats and pants—but we don't get them. When we sold our right to hunt [in the south] we did not expect to sell the ground; at least that was not told us.... The reason we accepted it was on account of white people going in there and killing the buffalos and throwing all the meat away.... [we wanted the money to buy wagons, horses and cows.... There will be cattle for issue here tomorrow, and I think they will be the best cattle in the herd, and I wish you would send someone to see the remainder of the herd.... There are a good many of the young men here who have been brought up among the whites, and they understand a good deal of the English language; they hear the people at the issuing cursing and swearing at them a good deal and we don't like that, and I hope you will have it stopped....[250]

After a few others reiterated the same or similar issues, the group retired until the evening when American Horse presided over a dance and feast for the visitors.

While no actual recording of the evening event exists, it probably involved as many as a hundred male Sioux whose faces and chests were painted with green and yellow stripes, red, white and blue stars, hand prints, spirals, zig-zags or other decorations. The dancers wore multiple bands of small bells resulting in an incredible noise as they circumnavigated the center of the gathering as drums maintained the

---

[250] Ibid.

beat. After the first dance, a leader—maybe Red Cloud or Sitting Bull—would have stepped to the center and welcomed the curious and slightly bewildered, white guests. Soon, a ceremonial bowl of stewed meat would have been brought by women to the Native-American host who would have taken a piece, said a prayer and put it into his mouth. Then bowls would have been passed to the guests and dances soon resumed. Few who attended would ever forget the evening.

The next day the commission reconvened and began to call witnesses. Eventually, over the next few days they listened to over one-hundred people. Only after any tribe member who wanted to speak had been heard did Fletcher move on. He wanted them to believe the commission really listen to them. This, would build trust.

The next task of the commission focused on the charges as submitted. Getting to the bottom of these issues would resolve the investigation. They essentially noted Professor Marsh's charges that included ten major allegations:

1. *J.J. Saville is "wholly unfit for his position and guilty of gross frauds upon the Indians in his charge."*
2. *The numbers of Indians were systematically overstated for purposes of fraud.*
3. *The last issue of annuity goods…suspicious, and, in part at least, fraudulent."*
4. *Inferior beef cattle were brought to the reservation.*
5. *The pork that was issued was not suitable for human food*
6. *The flour was very inferior*
7. *The "sugar and coffee were not good, although better than the other supplies."*
8. *The tobacco was rotten.*
9. *Our people suffered greatly during the past winter for want of food and clothing.*
10. *The freight contractor from Cheyenne paid for 212 miles when the actual mileage was 145.*[251]

---

[251] Ibid.

Agent Saville came before the commission and read a prepared response that essentially answered each charge.

1. *I MADE REPORTS COMPLETELY AND REGULARLY*
2. *There is resistance of the Indians to allow their correct number to be known. Reports show I have tried to be accurate.*
3. *The tribe got enough goods for the number reported; damages not my responsibility—contractors*
4. *I deny this*
5. *...prime pork, composed of shoulders and sides, cut up and put in together. As the Indians use pork mainly for the grease and did not understand how to cook this kind of pork, they cut off the fat and threw the lean away.... Indians felt unfit because of lean not because of bad quality*
6. *The flour was sent by contractors without inspection but I kept sample for review – it was ok; but the rest distributed before it could be inspected.*
7. *The sugar and coffee are okay*
8. *I didn't know about complaints about tobacco*
9. *This has been a hard winter: "That there was some suffering among the Indians at this agency last winter is not denied. The winter was excessively cold and the amount of clothing distributed to the Indians was not more than half enough for the number that were here to receive it. The amount of supplies, with the exception of been, was not sufficient.... (Congressional reduction of appropriations due to questions about over counting).*[252]

After the testimony of several witnesses and important contributors, Fletcher adjourned the hearings and began the third phase of his investigation.

The commission began looking into closely into each item of contention. Further, they also went to the Spotted Tail Indian Agency located about forty-five miles northeast of the Red Cloud Agency. They

---

[252] Ibid.

had also received the beef under question. Thus, this second agency fell under their purview. A principle leader in this reservation, Good Hawk, reiterated the same general complaints heard at the Red Cloud Agency but saved his primary attack for another issue. *"The white men are in the Black Hills just like maggots and I want you to get them out as quick as you can,"* he said, *"The chief of all thieves (General George A. Custer) made a road into the Black Hills last summer and I want the Great Father to pay damages for what Custer has done."*[253] Two Strike and Spotted Tail, while less adamant, still lamented about the inadequate funding for supplies allocated by the federal government.[254]

All did not go smoothly as the hearings continued. At one point, a large group of angry Native-Americans intent on killing Fletcher and the other commissioners had to be stopped and driven off by Sitting Bull's warriors. The warriors then surrounded the commissioners' compound to assure the continued safety of the group.[255] The U. S. Cavalry did not object and were not unhappy about their presence. The commission continued as if nothing had happened and did not mention the tense situation in their final report.

Among those called to testify was Rt. Reverend E.H. Hare, Bishop of Nebraska. The Red Cloud Agency lay in his diocese. Reverend Hare explained to the commission that Mr. Marsh had been mistaken about his perception of beef deliveries, a key issue of contention. According to the reverend, the discussion should not center on fraud but rather inadequacy.[256]

The investigation still continued to the end of September when Fletcher finally suggested to his friend, General Sherman, that they were ready *"...to go home,"* even though he had to make a speech at the Society of the Army of Tennessee first.[257] The investigation completed, the group broke up and returned east.

Fletcher did stop in Des Moines to make the principle address to

---

[253] *New York Daily Herald*, August 28, 1875, 4.

[254] Ibid.

[255] *Nebraska State Journal* (Lincoln, Nebraska), October 1, 1875, 2.

[256] *The Inter Ocean* (Chicago, Illinois), September 11, 1875, 9.

[257] *Baltimore Sun*, September 17, 1875, 1.

the veterans' group and on September 29th met with his friend, General Sherman.[258] At this meeting, Fletcher addressed the crowd as the first principle speaker. His sensitivity toward the national government and its detractors of the moment came through when he told the assembled former comrades, "...*this is a republic and a government by the people and of all the people, and not a government by the states and part of the people...*"[259] The *Inter Ocean* reporter described his address as "...*an eloquent effort delivered with very impressive effect.*"[260] Of concern to all of the day were the issues regarding Reconstruction. Southern states were rapidly returning to white rule and chafed at the federal occupation and the pro-African-American federal government. Many in the Southern states were again talking about "*States' Rights.*" At the same time, across the former rebel states' pro-whites were erecting statues to the "*heroes*" of the recent war. While superficially this effort seemed straight-forward, it also served to warn black citizens of the precariousness of their lives. So-called "*Redeemer Rule*" appeared just around the corner. Fletcher recognized these threats to the national union and would not stand idly by as they happened.

After his well-received speech and some enjoyable times with old friends, Fletcher immediately afterward traveled east to New York City. He wanted the report completed quickly as he had business at home in St. Louis. And, he missed his wife and family. Further, he still had railroad business and other legal issues demanding attention. One particularly important legal case he needed to deal with involved the famous St. Louis Whiskey Ring.

This famous scandal began in St. Louis but spread to Chicago, Milwaukee, Peoria, Indianapolis, Kansas City, and New Orleans. The owners of the Missouri *Globe Democrat*, William Mc Kee and Daniel Houser, had used their influence in the Republican Party to secure many patronage appointments. By 1871 they began systematically defrauding the government. They bribed governmental officials like John McDonald, supervisor of internal revenue for Missouri and the Southwest, and John A. Joyce, collector of revenue at St. Louis, to say

---

[258] *New York Daily Herold,* September 30, 1875, 7.
[259] *The Inter Ocean,* September 30, 1875, 1.
[260] Ibid.

that taxes paid at thirty-five cents a gallon had actually been paid at the required rate of seventy cents per gallon. Even President Grant's own secretary, Orville Babcock, participated in the scheme. By May, 1875, the scam had been illuminated and the notable Republicans were charged.[261] Fletcher, a life-long Republican, represented Arthur Guenther, a lower level participant and some others charged.[262] In fact, three years later, he approached President Grant on behalf of Mr. Henreichhoffen, Bernard Englee, Jno. L. Bernecker, A. M. Everst and Henry Hardaway, all of whom had been convicted for their respective parts in the Whiskey Ring. He secured their unconditional pardons.[263] The beginnings of this national scandal all bubbled up while Fletcher addressed the issues at the Red Cloud Agency far away from St. Louis.[264] There is nothing to explain the feelings of the ex-governor about representing these men. Likely, believing the even guilty men deserved the best defense before the bar, he used his skills in their defense. These skills were considerable.

At the end of the first week of October, 1875, Fletcher's commission continued hard at work at the Fifth Avenue Hotel in New York City attempting to complete the report. A particularly irksome issue centered around the beef sold to the Indians and complained about by them. The commission actually had cattle weighed and closely examined. No fraud was evident. They did, however, see inefficiencies and general gross mismanagement. A reporter noted that at a recent meeting with some members of the press, *"Governor Fletcher spoke very strongly on the management of Indian agencies and the general policy now in force,"* and noted that *"the Governor will probably furnish the Interior Department with some useful suggestions on the subject."*[265] He would do just that.

After the thorough investigation, an eight-hundred-page document found no actual fraud at the agency but proved great incompetency

---

[261] Parish, *History of Missouri, Vol. III,* 273-276; Primm, *Lion of the Valley,* 317-319.

[262] *New York Daily Herold,* January 19, 1876, 5.

[263] *Baltimore Sun,* November 8, 1878, 2.

[264] This corruption scandal tainted the Grant administration and supported many who believed Grant participate in the corruption; which he had not.

[265] *New York Daily Herold,* October 8, 1875, 1.

and gross neglect.[266] The report led to major changes at the site and provided great publicity for Fletcher's abilities.[267] Saville resigned before the final report could be announced. Fletcher concluded that Marsh's statements had not been accurate and might even have been libelous but he did not think Marsh had made the charges maliciously.[268] One of the most important recommendations asked that the *"future legislation be shaped with a view to bringing the Indians under the same laws which govern all the other inhabitants of the Republic."*[269] Marsh, himself, considered this effort *"to clear out the varmints"* as one of his life's most significant accomplishments.[270] One of Fletcher's great strengths was the ability to see both sides of issues. In this case his scathing report drew rapt attention from the Department of Justice as well as from other agencies of the Federal government.

Eventually, however, the tribe had to move even farther away from their native home; this time to the Pine Ridge Agency in South Dakota.[271] Fletcher's final report drew attention from across the country. Fletcher's name soon rose to the top of those who could be appointed the Director of Indian Affairs. While probably appreciating the attention and accolades, he likely did not want that job or any other governmental position. Working with the government could have been difficult enough; being part of the government might relegate him to obscurity and frustration. The publicity, however enhanced his value to those who would need assistance with Federal legal concerns. The demand for his services increased as a result of this effort. And, Tom would never forget the Native-Americans. Their hospitality, integrity, stoicism and callous

---

[266] *St. Louis Post-Dispatch,* October 19, 1875, 2.

[267] While improvements were made, the agency still saw much action when the Great Sioux War began in 1876. Young braves left the agency to join the resistance to white intrusions.

[268] *The Inter Ocean,* September 24, 1875, 5.

[269] *New York Daily Herald,* October, 1875, 6.

[270] Charles Schuchert, *"Biographical Memoir of Othneil Charles Marsh, 1831-1899,"* Presentation to the Academy at the annual meeting, 1938, 13.

[271] Marsh retained his friendship with Red Cloud afterward and later served as the president of the National Academy of Science.

mistreatment by unscrupulous and inept bureaucrats made him want to help them in the future.

Fletcher continued his interest in Native-American related issues throughout the remainder of his life and supported their appropriate treatment and legal rights. While Red Cloud stayed on the reservation after the report had some positive results, many of his young braves still left to follow Crazy Horse and Sitting Bull in their resistance to the *Indian Peace Policy* that provided them with inadequate living conditions and been a threat to their entire culture. In June, 1876, this all came to a head when an expedition attempted to remove the recalcitrant Native-Americans in the Powder River country—if they could locate them. The arrogant Lieutenant Colonel George Armstrong Custer found them first. He led almost two-hundred men of the 7th Cavalry to their unnecessary death at the famous or infamous "Battle of the Little Big Horn." Learning of this event, Fletcher felt disgusted with the defeat. As a military man, he certainly grieved for the soldiers whose bodies were found scattered across the field of battle. He likely had little use for Custer and may have agreed with the negative assessment of the famous Custer by many in the military and by some of Fletcher's Republican friends. Although working on numerous legal issues, Fletcher discussed the disaster with many of his friends. Upon a visit to Washington D. C. the discussions continued with military and political friends there. *"Who was to blame?"* became the favorite and frequent argument in the capital city. Fletcher probably had his own military-based opinion regarding the battle tactics or lack thereof. But, it really didn't matter much because, the real blame, Fletcher believed, certainly rested at least in major part on the government's shoulders. He disgustedly told a *New York Herald* reporter who had buttonholed him and a few of his friends, *"...the present deplorable state of affairs ('Custer's Last Stand') has, without a shadow of a doubt, been brought about by the present peace policy of the government."*[272] His frank assessment may not have been received well by many in government, but Fletcher had put his finger on the real issue: *What was the best way to deal with indigenous people*

---

[272] *New York Daily Herald,* July 7, 1876, 4.

that had lived in the nation since before recorded time and now stood in front of the westward expansion of the new dominant culture? The correct answer eluded him.

He also focused attention to other Native-American groups after this experience. Especially important to him were the *"Five Civilized Tribes"* as they lived adjacent to Missouri in *"Indian Territory."*[273] These formerly southeastern Indian tribes included the *Seminole, Cherokee, Chickasaw, Choctaw, and Creek* (Muscogee). They had been removed from their homes and resettled in the Oklahoma Territory in a series of movements along the *"Trail of Tears"* in the 1830's. During the Civil War the tribes had split over alliances with Confederates and the Federal government. After the war, the Federal government assured them security from white intrusion. This empty promise, like many others, did little to solve problems. The land in Indian Territory had little value for the most part.[274] However, the areas in the northern section near Kansas and Missouri were attractive to white settlers and to railroads. Friction ensued especially along an area known as the "Cherokee Strip."

In 1880, Fletcher began the project that would take him over ten years to complete: organizing the Cherokee Strip land negotiations. He first secured forty thousand dollars from Congress (*about nine-hundred-thousand dollars in 2018*) to open federal land offices in "No Man's Land," the area under scrutiny for future development. He also arranged for the release of a significant amount of tribal funds held by the federal government *"in-trust"* for them. The government had given the Delawares, who lived with the Cherokees, a substantial financial settlement but did not trust them to spend it wisely. Thus, they kept it *"in trust."* Fletcher successfully intervened on their behalf to obtain release of the needed funds.[275] Later in his career he led the legal efforts to establish a reasonable solution to the problem of how to settle the Cherokee Strip land issue.[276] While this issue took several years and extensive work

---

[273] *Washington Post,* (Washington D. C.) December 21, 1890. 1.

[274] The land later was found to have some of the largest oil reserves in the nation.

[275] *Wichita Daily Eagle* (Wichita, Kansas), June 14, 1880, 1.

[276] *Muskogee Phoenix,* (Muskogee, Oklahoma), May 22, 1890.

with the congress and the Supreme Court, once a settlement had been agreed to, Fletcher received a significant financial settlement in 1893. This assured comfort in his old age.[277] Because of Fletcher, the Native-Americans received just compensation for a land takeover that would happen regardless of their best interests.

---

[277] *St. Louis Post Dispatch,* July 1, 1893, 1.

Politics, Veterans, and
Washington D.C.

few years after his trip to the Red Cloud Indian agency in 1875,
Fletcher agreed to step back into politics a bit in St. Louis.
He worked for the Republican Party candidates and for other
political issues in the 1876 election—an uphill effort. Ohio's Republican
governor, Rutherford B. Hayes secured the presidency only after much
drama and the Senate Republicans agreeing to end Reconstruction. The
African-Americans in the United States were the ones who really lost in
this election. In Missouri, the Republican Party had effectively split into
Liberal and Conservative branches. Fletcher had used all his influence
to gain support for Grant in his 1872 re-election campaign and still held
great respect among the leadership and rank and file of the Party in 1876.
But, by that year, the Missouri Republican Party had begun a downhill
spiral.

After much pressure, Fletcher reluctantly accepted the party's
nomination for the Third District U.S. congressional seat four years
later in 1880. Republican James A. Garfield appeared likely to win the
presidency. But, the former slave states, Missouri included, had turned
more toward the Democratic Party. Popular Democrat Thomas T.
Crittenden seemed poised to win the governor's seat and actually did

so.[278] In order to win anywhere in Missouri a widely respected person would have to be selected by the Republicans for the contested seat. The party thought Fletcher's support from the African-American community and moderate—almost bi-partisan—nature might be enough to sway the congressional district election in their favor. The strong German support still looked good to Fletcher. St Louis still had a large immigrant population, led by Germans. The rise of the Greenback Party, a *"third party"* that had limited appeal among labor could influence the final results of any particularly close election. In this election it proved to be a negative "wild card" for the Republicans; at least for Fletcher. Fletcher may also have been tainted by the Grant Administration's corruption regardless of the fact that he had nothing to do with it. He still carried the *"Republican"* label. And, in reality, Democrats and "Redeemer Rule" had fully returned in Missouri. Fletcher could not succeed. Even though he would continue to speak to and support Republicans in the State and city, he never ran again for any office.

Regardless of his political, veteran, and legal activities throughout his life after the governorship, Fletcher continued involvement with many diverse organizations and causes. As a prominent resident of St. Louis, he focused much on the city's improvement. National magazine *The Ladies' Repository* described Fletcher, *"As a public man Governor Fletcher identifies himself with very movement whose object is the improvement of the material and social interests of the people. He is always ready at any expense of personal convenience to address a railroad meeting, a Board of Trade, a teachers' convention, a literary association, or a Sunday school, actuated by the principle that every man is bound to contribute what he can to the good of society."*[279] He loved St. Louis and continued to work for its betterment throughout the remainder of his life. Music and art remained important to both him and Clara. Perhaps because of his wife's interest in the arts, he became an acquaintance of the famous entertainer, comedian and philanthropist, Lotta Crabtree. He intervened on behalf of her when her

---

[278] Missouri would not only elect Crittenden, in 1884 former senior Confederate Cavalry Officer, John Sappington Marmaduke, would be elected governor.

[279] "Fletcher," *Ladies' Repository*, 365.

father stole some of her property, including a significant amount of cash. His efforts allowed her to continue on her travels.[280]

He also served as the business manager of the St. Louis Academy of Music and Gallery of Art.[281] Clara, also stayed busy. She served on the governing board of the Women's Christian Association that supported women's housing, health, education and other needs. She also worked on the Women's Centennial Organization that helped plan St. Louis' celebration of the one hundredth anniversary of the founding of the nation. Fletcher echoed her interest in education and made speeches supporting public investment in education.[282] In 1869 he visited Atchison, Topeka, Lawrence and Leavenworth to support the fund-raising efforts of the Educational and Industrial Institute of Kansas which provided advanced education for African-Americans who lived in Topeka and the surrounding area. He had not forgotten black Americans.

He avoided one event even though his brothers, John William Fletcher and Major Charles Carroll Fletcher, apparently willingly participated despite being strong Republicans. Former Confederate President Jefferson Davis visited De Soto in the early fall of 1875, as part of his swing across the south and former border states to support "*redeemer rule.*"[283] This appears to have been be an attempt to foster reconciliation between former rebels and the pro-Union citizens of De Soto and Jefferson County. At the time of this questionable celebration, Thomas delivered the introductory speech at the annual Convention of the Army of Tennessee in Iowa and introduced the key-note speaker, President Ulysses S. Grant.[284]

Fletcher felt content to stay in the background on most political issues, giving his support to the Republican Party as appropriate after the failure in 1876. The Republican St. Louis city leadership known as the "Committee of Twenty-eight" and the "Committee of Ten" frequently

---

[280] *Richmond Dispatch,* June 2, 1868, 2.

[281] *St. Louis Post Dispatch*, May 4, 1874, 4.

[282] *Atchison Daily Champion* (Atchison, Kansas), April 6, 1869, 3.

[283] *Atchison Daily Champion*, September 8, 1875, 1.

[284] *Baltimore Sun*, October 1, 1875, 1.

met in Fletcher's office in the late 1870's and early 1880's.[285] Even in Washington D.C. his presence was felt. He helped create the tongue-in-cheek organization of Missouri Senators, Representatives and others known as the *"Missouri State Association"* that appeared to be more social than political.[286] Cigars, brandy and great conversation (*often of a political nature*) appeared to be the group's primary interest. But, their meetings warranted a mention in many newspapers. He found time to work with the St. Louis City Southwestern Improvement Association regarding city roads, bridges, railroad and streetcar concerns.[287] His law practice took up most of his time. But there were exceptions.

Of particular concern to the former governor were military and veterans' issues. He had seen the best of men die right next to him. He suffered with them in prison camps. He had led men who, in following him, offered their lives for their common cause. After the war, he saw great military men try to adjust to a new difficult reality. *Post-Traumatic Stress Disorder* (PTSD) existed, even if there were no such diagnoses at this point in history. In addition, many former servicemen had become addicted to opiates and had to deal with the medical and psychological issues without the benefit of modern understanding and treatment. In addition to the problems that drew attention, there was a camaraderie that Fletcher felt with these men that few outside the military could understand.

He belonged to the St. Louis based General Lyon Post of The Grand Army of the Republic (G.A.R.), the largest association of Union Civil War Veterans. This St. Louis branch of the national organization aligned closely with the national organization. The national G.A.R. founded soldiers' homes, provided relief efforts, supported white veterans along with blacks and had significant political influence within the Republican Party.

He also belonged to the *Loyal Legion* and the *Society of the Army of the Tennessee*. The Loyal Legion had been established after the assassination of Lincoln. It created a permanent organization of officers and former

---

[285] Ibid., September 27, 1882, 2.
[286] *National Republican* (Washington, District of Columbia), February 8, 1870, 4.
[287] *St. Louis Post Dispatch,* February 25, 1888, 3.

officers patterned after the Society of Cincinnati established after the Revolutionary War. It formed to protect the national government, to honor the memories of Union army veterans, assist veterans as needed, care for veterans' widows and orphans and to provide opportunities to meet with other officers in fraternal fellowship.

Among his veteran-related activities, his membership in the *Society of the Army of Tennessee* brought him great pride. General Sherman said of the Army of the Tennessee that it *"never checked—always victorious; so rapid in motion—so eager to strike; it deserved its name of the 'Whiplash,' swung from one flank to the other, as danger called, night or day, sunshine or storm."*[288] Fletcher remembered his own participation in the travails of the army. Throughout the rest of his life Fletcher attended and frequently addressed thousands of participants at various veterans' meetings all over the north and northeast states. He frequently chaired the celebrations. These annual meetings rotated around the country to generate interest and participation. While St. Louis often hosted them, Milwaukie, Cincinnati, Chicago, Washington D. C., and New York also played host. General Sherman attended almost every one held until his death. Fletcher attended as many as he could. In the first twenty years after the war the attendees held rallies for veterans, considered possible legislation related to veteran interests and assisted veterans in need. By the late 1880's they became more social in nature as the numbers diminished through deaths among its membership. Of course, they could always provide an *"honor guard"* when the president of the United States or some other major dignitary wanted them.

Even low-ranking soldiers who got in trouble could count on General Fletcher. In 1878, he assisted a veteran (*a former musician*) of the Army of the Tennessee who had been convicted of murder. The man had done *"all he did for the love of a woman."*[289] Although sentenced to hang, Fletcher had the sentence commuted to five years in prison. His influence and powers of persuasion must have been something spectacular to obtain this change in sentence.

---

[288] As quoted in "Army of Tennessee," *Wikipedia.*

[289] *New York Daily Herald,* (New York City, New York), October 18, 1878, 1.

Fletcher also provided memorial speeches at the funerals of many military leaders including those of Grant and Sherman. He remained extremely close to Sherman throughout the general's life after the war. Upon the death of the great general, Fletcher wrote about those who attended his funeral, "... *a half million of people, of every party, sect and nationality— men, women and children— stood uncovered, and thousands*

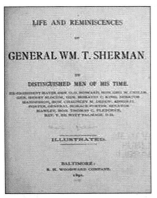

Life and Reminiscences of General William T. Sherman, written and compiled by General Thomas C. Fletcher, 1891; Public Domain.

wept as the cortège moved to the cemetery, all moved by a feeling not only that he was the greatest military chieftain at his death in all the world, but because he was esteemed by them as a kindhearted, social, benevolent friend, whom they had learned to love in their social contact with him."[290] As a final tribute to the noted general, Fletcher compiled reminisces about him from former officers, politicians and President Hayes. In 1891, he published the compilation as *Life and Reminiscences of General Wm. T. Sherman.* Fletcher probably was included in the numbers of St. Louisians whose largesse provided a home for Sherman and financial support in his later years. Fletcher understood honor, duty and loyalty.

To one meeting of the Army of the Tennessee, Fletcher in 1872, as key note speaker, spoke of the Army of the Ohio that had supported his troops at the Battle of Lookout Mountain, "...*it formed a part of that long line whose glittering bayonets we saw from the summit of Lookout Mountain as it stretched across the valley... It perhaps never before and never will be again permitted any men to behold so grand a sight as that....*"[291] Throughout the remainder of his life veteran's issues remained on the center of his plate.

The "Indian Question" also continued off and on with Fletcher and haunted the nation. Apache raids, Sioux extra-reservation actions, public outcry on behalf or against the indigenous people boiled over

---

[290] *Life and Reminiscences*, xvi.
[291] *The Inter Ocean*, July 8, 1872, 2.

in conversations across the nation. Reporters often sought Fletcher for a response to some issue or another. His frustration sometimes showed. In the beginning of the summer of 1883, perhaps on railroad business in southern Arkansas, a discussion about what to do with Native-Americans began with some friends and acquaintances. When a reporter from Arkansas who happened to be there asked him about the latest "problem", he voiced a tongue-in-cheek solution, "*The true and practical way of dealing with the savage tribes is to plant them east of the Mississippi and in the very middle of civilization, instead of fencing them off from it as is now done. It would be cheaper to feed and clothe them in the East, cost of lands, etc. included.*"[292] *The Southern Standard*, an Arkansas newspaper, printed this somewhat flippant or at least frustrated response to the inadequate federal Indian Policy on the front page of the weekend newspaper. Wherever he went people sought his advice or illumination.

---

[292] *The Southern Standard* (Arkadelphia, Arkansas), July 21, 1883, 1.

Private Citizen, the Later Years

T homas Fletcher continued to be respected in both St. Louis and in the national capital as he grew older. The *Bench and Bar* publication of 1884 noted that *"He became one of the most learned and efficient members of the legal profession."*[293] In matters of patronage in the West, President Harrison often sought his input. Other presidents, cabinet members and elected officials also listened to him. Often, particularly significant occurrences involved Fletcher intervening on behalf of a former soldier with President Cleveland. Normally, such involvement surprised few. In one case, however, it involved a former rebel officer.

Former Confederate General, Joseph O. Shelby, had been appointed to the office of U. S. Marshal of the Western District of Missouri sometime after the Democrats regained the governor's office and controlled most of the legislature. President Cleveland had rescinded the appointment due to pressure from many who still abhorred any former Confederate soldier. One valid criticism had been that Shelby was the only Confederate General that had never surrendered at the end of the war. He fled to Mexico and then later returned—but never surrendered. Fletcher believed that the opposition to the old general's appointment

---

[293] *Bench and Bar,* 282.

had been political and mean-spirited. The past did not determine the man's current life, Fletcher generously decided. He intervened for him with the president. Cleveland then reinstated the general. Of perhaps only historical interest, during the Civil War Shelby had once led rebel troops in an assault directly against Fletcher's own Federal brigade in a battle near Atlanta.[294]

In 1885, An anomalous and mysterious event also resulted in great interest about Fletcher. It perplexed him for a long time. It began simple enough. On a routine business matter for the Iron Mountain Railroad in Farmington, Missouri, he received a telegram calling him to Matamoras, Mexico on urgent business (*the nature of which he never revealed*). On March 28, 1885, he gave a dispatch to a railroad conductor to be forwarded to his wife informing her of his intention to immediately leave on this unanticipated trip. Unknown to him, and for unexplained reasons, the message did not arrive. Clara expected him home and became distraught when he didn't arrive at the expected time. Very shortly thereafter, within a couple of days, she contacted friends and then reached out to the *St. Louis Post Dispatch*. Telegrams flew across Missouri to friends and acquaintances to see if any information about his whereabouts could be learned. Due to his national stature and importance, very shortly almost a hundred newspapers across the country joined in the search for the "*missing*" or "*lost governor*." As with such public searches at any time, "*sightings*" were announced from all over. He was seen in Kansas City on a train. He tried to borrow two-thousand dollars from a businessman. He had dyed his hair white but left his beard black and was seen wandering around. He gave evidence of mental illness to several who had surely observed him. He had donned the clothes of a homeless derelict and ambled around aimlessly. He had checked in to a hotel in Colorado but left shortly thereafter. He had telegraphed home for money because he was strapped. And, so on....

In fact, telegrams were also sent by military officials in St. Louis to military bases across the west to ask for their help to find him. On April 3rd, only five days after he "went missing," he arrived in Laredo, Texas,

---

[294] *Albany Ledger* (Albany, Missouri), March 31, 1899, 3.

on his return from Mexico. His appearance made headlines across the country. *"The governor was greatly surprised to find that he had been written up in the newspapers,"* noted the *Topeka Daily Capital*.[295] The *St. Louis Post Dispatch* noted the ex-governor was *"exceedingly annoyed at the sensation which his absence has caused."*[296]

For weeks thereafter, almost a hundred newspapers reported on the strange set of circumstances surrounding the national news-media event Most just reprinted the same story. Some commented, with tongue in cheek, about the *"lost governor of Missouri."* Complicating the absence, the first confirmed reconnection had arrived via telegraph from a Lieut. Byrnes attached to General David Sloan Stanley out of San Antonio's garrison at Fort Sam Houston. This only stirred more speculation at the time. Stanley and Fletcher had served together during the Atlanta Campaign during the Civil War. Stanley, like Fletcher, had worked well with the Native-American tribes, maintaining peaceful relations. In 1885, the General commanded the second largest fort in the United States. Speculation about the development of a railroad line reaching from St. Louis to the port of Matamoras suggests that Fletcher may have been on an exploratory effort to evaluate this possibility or to deal with some obstacle. Fletcher's influence with the Native-American population in Oklahoma and Stanley's with those of West Texas and New Mexico might have figured into a possible railroad right-of-way discussion with entrepreneurs in Mexico. In fact, only a few years later a railroad line from St. Louis to Matamoras did get built. But, there might also have been some reason that the ex-governor had to go to Painted Rock near Austin Texas. Fetcher's daughter reportedly lived on a ranch near there. Her marriage might have been on a shaky foundation due to her husband's known volatility and her father might have wanted to see her. The fact is, no reason for the "business trip," ever came to light. But the attention to Fletcher's comings and goings to many across the nation did not hurt his fame. He probably later had quite a few interesting discussions with his

---

[295] *The Topeka Daily Capital* (Topeka, Kansas), April 4, 1885, 4.
[296] *St. Louis Post Dispatch* (St. Louis, Missouri) April 4, 1885, 2.

friends in Washington D.C. and St. Louis about this event. Upon arriving back home, his discussion with Clara could also have been fascinating.

Throughout many of Fletcher's travels, his wife, Clara, remained in St. Louis at their home at 1819 Minnesota Avenue. While Tom traveled much of the time, her family and many friendships remained solidly entrenched in St. Louis and back in De Soto. There was much for her and her family to do in the exciting city of St. Louis. The "Gateway to the West" had matured in many ways. In 1874, the Eads Bridge brought Illinois and Missouri only a few minutes apart. As the newly emerged raw cotton center for the United States, the city's economic base grew. Civic improvements that Clara probably supported also prospered with the influx of funds. In 1876 the separation of the City from the County allowed the effective and innovative utilization of copious city tax revenues. Forest Park soon came into existence and the city expanded to surround it. Suburbs like Wellston, Normandy and Florissant grew, attached by rail to the city centers. Now, social clubs like Glen Echo Country Club (*the first golf club west of the Mississippi*) began to develop. Other social centers of St. Louis boasted great opera, riveting theater productions and boisterous musicals throughout the various venues. Clara would have participated in many of these and certainly financially supported many. As the wife of the former governor, Clara found herself sought by many private boards and service organizations. She joined the ones she felt strongest about.

As with most women of the more affluent classes, Clara maintained an active social life. One event brought newspaper attention. She hosted an open house on New Year's Day, 1886. Society demanded such actions by the more elite of the city. On New Year's Day, Clara brought together her daughter, Ella Bartholow, and friends Mrs. G.D. Reynolds and Mrs. W.S. Reife to meet their guests. Visitors would leave their cards in hope of reciprocity at another time. The hostesses offered tea, cookies and small cakes and sometimes small cucumber sandwiches artfully arranged on silver and crystal platters that would dazzle the visitors. Of course, each lady would wear their finest clothes. Clara had learned to make a life for herself and reveled in her daughter's presence. She represented her husband well and with grace.

Clara's husband continued his law practice and used his political influence in the capital, traveling back and forth from St. Louis. As the change of administration occurred in 1889, his position in the Republican Party gave him access to the incoming president, Benjamin Harrison. Fletcher spent quite a bit of time with the new president and predicted that James G. Blaine would certainly be picked for Secretary of State "beyond a doubt." His pick for Postmaster General, John Wanamaker was also spot-on.[297] His own name came up for many cabinet positions and even for the Governor of Utah or Ambassador to Austria. While he enjoyed the attention, Fletcher appears to have had little interest in serving in the government; he still liked being of service to it. Fletcher probably had at least some influence in the expansion of ex-soldiers' and federal workers' pensions and the creation of additional medical care in veterans' hospitals. Harrison, a man of integrity, had served in the Union Army and openly shared Fletcher's support for African-American rights. The two shared common interests in advancing the cause of African-American economic, political and social development regardless of Southern antagonism toward those goals. During Harrison's administration, six western states entered the Union: North Dakota, South Dakota, Montana, Washington, Idaho and Wyoming. His legislature, sometimes called "the Billion-Dollar Congress" focused much on economic development. This spending spree resulted in Grover Cleveland returning to the presidency in 1892. But, while Harrison sat in the White House, Fletcher had great influence. Even later, President Grover Cleveland paid attention to him during each of his own terms.

Turning back to Native-American affairs in 1889, he presided over a joint conference of tribal representatives from Indian Territory and whites from Missouri to create a regular territorial government. He believed that Indian Territory "*is as effectual a hiding place for criminals as Canada.*"[298] This conference, held in Fort Smith, Arkansas, as part of "The Indian Territorial Convention," drew representatives from all the "Civilized Tribes" and cities as far away as Memphis, Tennessee, St. Louis

---

[297] *Pittsburgh Daily Post* (Pittsburgh, Pennsylvania), January 28, 1889, 2.
[298] Ibid.

and Kansas City, Missouri and Galveston, Texas. Fletcher provided the evening's major result: the memorial or petition to congress from the assembled group. His petition set forth that the Indian Territory "...*is an anomaly in the United States and its political and tribal status area an obstruction to civilization and detrimental to the Indians, rendering their land tenure insecure and their condition one of semi-barbarity...* (it further set forth) *the necessity for the enforcement of the obligations of property rights between Whites...* (and protecting the rights of the Indians) *to allot them their lands in severalty and invest them with their full rights under treaty obligations.*[299] This petition followed the goals of many in congress to revamp the national relations with indigenous populations. Fletcher evidently supported the creation of a new approach as he knew the current policy had only proved disastrous.

A few days later he led a delegation back to Washington D. C. to support the Taos Valley Company to help them get an appropriation for the Taos Valley in New Mexico and Colorado to build a canal to supply the people with water.[300] This would assist Native-American and white farmers. He continued to effectively assist with tribal allotment issues as they popped up, traveling through Missouri, Kansas, Oklahoma, Texas, New Mexico and other areas as needed. In 1890, he put his negotiating and legal skills to use as he again represented the Delaware tribe in the Cherokee Nation in a serious concern they had with the federal government.

In 1887 The Dawes Act effectively reduced Native-American tribal land holdings throughout the West and substituted individual land allotments to individuals. Its implementation met with great resistance. Eventually, it served as the guide for most reservations across the west. Massachusetts Senator Henry Laruen Dawes had introduced this bill for the most noble of intentions; even if naïve in reality. The act first called for Indian lands to be surveyed. The government then divided the tribal land among the individual families based on a formula related to the *"best land use capability."* The *"surplus"* or *"excess land"* resultant from

---

[299] *Abilene Daily Reflector* (Abilene, Kansas), January 25, 1889, 1.
[300] *Pittsburgh Daily Post*, January 28, 1889, 2.

this reallocation could then be disposed of by the government. Indian families would be interspersed among the whites who would then come in to the area to purchase the *"surplus"* or *"excess land."* Those Native-Americans who accepted this and moved away from the tribe would then be enfranchised and entitled to all the rights and responsibilities of any citizen (at least in theory).[301] In 1890 after the plan's implementation had been initiated, the Washington D.C. *Evening Star,* clearly demonstrated the situation as it related to one small tribe: the Sisseton Indian Tribe of western Minnesota. This tribe, friendly to Lewis and Clark, and one of the smaller tribes of the Dakota Sioux, had always lived a mixed life of maize cultivation and buffalo hunting. By 1862, they had resigned themselves to reservation life albeit with some excursions by some of the younger warriors in futile acts of rebellion. The 1890 article described the plan under which the Sissetons would have to live.

> There are about 1,500 Indians on the reservation... and allotting them 160 acres a head there are 700,000 acres to be thrown open for settlement.... the agreement... allows them $2.50 an acre for all lands thrown open (to be put in trust for the tribe). It also provided that settlers shall pay $2.50 an acre for the lands (so) there is really no expense to the government.
>
> The lands being surrounded by an improved country ought to be worth more than that and... speculators (might) gobble it up....
>
> ... the lands might sell at auction for $5 an acre, and so far as we are concerned, a speculator is not much better than an Indian.
>
> ...(the Native-Americans) are to be scattered around among the settlers. That is the only solution of the Indian question. They have been there since 1851, when it was a wild frontier with many dangers, but now, with civilization all around them, it is time for the tribal relation to be broken

---

[301] Native-Americans could not vote in the United States until 1924.

up and the lands occupied and tilled. The earth was theirs,
but the fullness thereof comes only with the White man.[302]

The funds realized from the forced sale of these Sisseton lands, like those of other tribes, were placed in trust for the Native-American individuals. The federal government's Department of the Interior would manage and disperse the funds as appropriate. But, in order to receive the proceeds from their own federal trust, the entire tribe had to be declared *"enlightened and progressive."* The government continued to treat the Native-Americans as *"wards"* and would act in their best interests for them. After all, the government knew what was best.

In the case of the Delaware tribe, the Secretary of the Interior did not believe they had met the government standards and had refused to release their funds. The tribe turned to the one man they trusted who had any influence, Thomas C. Fletcher. Tom once again used his influence with the government (*this time directly with Senator Henry Dawes*) to get the decision reversed. In 1890, the tribe received almost four hundred and sixty thousand dollars (almost eleven million dollars in 2018 dollars) and Fletcher's fee amounted to about forty thousand dollars (almost nine hundred thousand dollars in 2018 dollars) which he split with Chief Johnnycake of the Delawares.[303] Whether or not Fletcher felt he could stop this largely successful attempt to steal Indian land or not, he worked within the system to assist those affected by it as best as he could. He had a strong sense of justice—but understood political realities.

In 1892, part of his past came back to the foreground. A seemingly unimportant event after the Battle of Pilot Knob bubbled to the surface. Attempting to evade Price's advance guard after the battle, part of Fletcher's command, exhausted and hungry, stopped at the boarding house of Peter Martin. Martin, a loyal Irishman, willingly fed them and provided a place for a short rest before their continuing their orderly retreat and rear-guard protection for the main column. The federal troops left little behind once they had proceeded on the march toward

---

[302] *Evening Star* (Washington D.C.), February 18, 1890, 9.
[303] *St. Louis Post Dispatch*, June 12, 1890, 2.

Rolla. Martin had not asked Fletcher for a voucher to pay for the support and *"Fletcher was probably too much in a hurry to think of it himself."* When the war ended, Martin submitted a bill for $77.50 to the government. Somehow or another, payment did not follow. The matter, evidently, faded into the past. But, in 1892, Missouri Congressman, O'Neill decided to go to Fletcher to get some help. Fletcher remembered the event vividly and made an affidavit supporting the bill. Martin shortly received his payment; twenty-eight years late.[304] Fletcher's name continued to generate respect in the national capital.

One of the last major unique efforts Fletcher undertook took him to congress and New York. It required him to use all of his personal abilities, political and personal influence. A world's fair (Columbian Exposition) would be held in the United States in 1893. St. Louis citizens and leadership wanted it to be held in their city. But a case could be made for Kansas City, Chicago, New York or even Washington D.C. itself. Once St. Louis supporters had raised five thousand dollars they were ready to begin lobbying efforts in Washington D.C. They just needed the right leader for the delegation. Of course, they chose Thomas C. Fletcher.[305]

He lost no time. Just a few weeks after being selected to lead the delegation, he and Missouri Governor David Roland Francis spoke to The Business Men's Club in Washington D. C. The Washington paper *Evening Star* wrote that Fletcher *"gave expression to the hopes which had brought him to this city by saying that the world's fair should be held in St. Louis and that Washington should aid the movement."* The article noted that *"The members of the club smiled audibly at this audacious proposition."*[306] Just a few weeks later in St. Louis as he prepared for another trip to the Capital, Fletcher told the crowd, *"St. Louis will get the Fair to a certainty, of that I feel perfectly confident.... A great many congressmen will vote first for New York who really support St. Louis.... They cannot gracefully come out for St. Louis at first... but when the real pull comes will be in the ranks of St.*

---

[304] *Ironton County Register* (Ironton, Missouri), January 14, 1892, 6.

[305] *St. Louis Post-Dispatch*, November 13, 1889, 4.

[306] *Evening Star*, November 21, 1889, 3.

Louis.... Unless something unforeseen occurs when we come back the World's Fair will be assured for St. Louis."[307]

On a stop in Pittsburgh, Fletcher encouraged Pennsylvania's support for St. Louis' bid for the fair. He noted that if the award went to St. Louis, Pittsburgh would see more people passing through it than if other locations were chosen. He also suggested that St. Louis would turn to Pittsburgh for iron and glass for the buildings to be built for the fair.[308] Pittsburgh Plate Glass had already strong ties to St. Louis as it had a significant financial interest in the Crystal City glass works located only a few miles from the ex-governor's home town in Jefferson County, Missouri. After the successful stopover, the delegation went on to New York City to meet with the most influential people they could find.

A week later, the *Evening Star* took notice of Fletcher's meeting with the New York World's Fair Delegation that included Democrat New York Mayor Hugh Grant, Cornelius Vanderbilt, Elihu Root and others."[309] Unfortunately, something unforeseen did occur. It derailed all the St. Louis delegation's efforts. A financial scandal involving the Missouri State Treasurer hit the news while they were in Washington D. C. This embarrassed the committee members and cast doubt on St. Louis' chances. Governor Francis had to return to Jefferson City to do damage control. The timing destroyed the effort to get the fair in St. Louis. However, this effort still set the stage for the later successful crusade to obtain the World's Fair in 1904.[310]

Although unsuccessful in this effort, his relationships in Washington D.C. continued to bear fruit. While the new president, Grover Cleveland, appreciated Fletcher and would talk with him, Fletcher focused mostly on cabinet and department personnel when matters of concern came up. Fletcher continued working in Washington D. C. on behalf of friends or clients seeking potential appointments in one department or another. Of course, he still took cases to the U. S. Supreme Court and provided

---

[307] *St. Louis Post-Dispatch,* January 5, 1890, 8.

[308] *Pittsburg Daily Post* (Pittsburgh, Pennsylvania), January 6, 1890.

[309] *Evening Star,* January 13, 1890, 8.

[310] Harper Barnes, *Standing on a Volcano: The Life and Times of David Rowland Francis,* Missouri Historical Society Press (Saint Louis), 2001, 74-75.

general legal counsel to his many friends. And, he did not let his law practice interfere with his support for other causes. Frequently meeting with Democratic President Grover Cleveland and then Republican Benjamin Harrison and then Cleveland again, Fletcher became known as the man to go to from Missouri.[311] His influence spread beyond those from Missouri, however. He became much in demand throughout the national capital. These demands soon overtook his ability to divide his time between St. Louis and Washington D. C. A choice needed to be made. Clara, still very close to her daughter probably only reluctantly agreed to leave Missouri. She may have arranged with her husband to support her desire to spend extended visits in St. Louis. They decided to move.

Shortly after the Fletchers left for Washington D. C., the *St. Louis Post Dispatch* noted how important Fletcher had been in St. Louis. "...*he was always good natured [and still firm and inflexible] during his long residence in St. Louis... [and] achieved as many Democratic as Republican friends.*"[312]

---

[311] *Pittsburg Dispatch*, (Pittsburgh, Pennsylvania) July 15, 1889, 2.

[312] *St. Louis Post Dispatch*, March 14, 1889, 1.

Private Citizen, The Last Years in D.C.

Fletcher and his wife moved to the capital city in early 1890. They leased rooms at 1327 N street northwest (*Historic District of the Logan Circle neighborhood today*) rather than buying property. They chose a magnificent 1860's row house with an Italianate bay facing the street containing a setback entrance. The upper-middle class residence served their purposes well. The prospect of continued travel back and forth from St. Louis as he aged might have caused Tom some health concerns in addition to the inconvenience. Although only sixty-three, he suffered from lung issues. His energy level had also diminished a bit. His new home lay only seven blocks from the U. S. capital. Streetcars passed almost directly by his front door. He might have realized that as he aged, ill health could be dealt with and his business interrupted as little as possible if he lived in the capital city. Perhaps linked to the incarceration in Libby Prison and subsequent lung-related illnesses thereafter, Fletcher continually battled pneumonia throughout his life. His susceptibility to the incapacitating illness had only increased as he aged. Beginning in his early sixties, Tom found long trips physically difficult to undertake. And, increasingly, his legal practice involved the federal government in some way or another. Never ostentatiously wealthy, Tom and Clara could not just retire and live off their investments. Logic declared that they rent for a while, at least until their finances allowed the purchase of something else. While certainly not likely to starve, they did have to watch their expenses.

In their new location, Tom and Clara could easily walk between Logan Circle with the statue of Fletcher's Civil War commanding officer and close friend, General John A. Logan, and the Thomas Circle named after another colleague, General Henry Thomas (*"The Rock of Chickamauga"*). In many evenings he and his wife would often do just that; still holding hands as they strolled along. Clara would receive visitors on Tuesdays but really still missed her daughter and St. Louis friends. She often found herself alone as Tom worked late into the night; often away from home. The ex-Governor spent long days and many evenings in the political arena as more business got taken care of in hotel lobbies or upscale establishments than in congressional offices. Smoke-filled lobbies and brandy facilitated the dealings. And throughout the 1890's there was much for Tom to be concerned about and some to deal with. Not the least of his anxieties were the resurgence of Jim Crow laws across the South. This probably brought great sadness to Fletcher, whose life had always been dedicated to giving a voice to those who had no voice.

Clara dealt with this as best as she could but then began to return to St. Louis probably more often than her husband wanted. She began to spend extended periods of time with Ella at the 1819 Minnesota Ave home in St. Louis. But Ella's husband's government positions also often required moving about. For a short period of time, her daughter, Francis Ella Bartholow, with her husband, Perry, had lived in Germany. He served as the United States Consul in Mayence, Germany. After a significant diplomatic *faux pas*, Perry moved back to St. Louis.[313] Of course Clara missed her and continued being as active as possible in the national capital. When Ella returned, Clara then often spent months with her daughter in St. Louis while her husband attended to business In Washington D.C..[314]

Regardless of other business, Fletcher always had time for veterans.

---

[313] *St. Louis Post Dispatch* (St. Louis, Missouri), January 29, 1897, 3; Perry Bartholow's "quick temper" resulted in a fine of two-hundred Marks for his assault of a household servant.

[314] *Evening Star,* November 26, 1890, 2.

As he now lived in the capital, he could certainly attend many military and veteran-related events; he did just that. He made speeches at most G.A.R. meetings and other veterans' conventions and meetings. At the reunion of the seventh army corps on Sept 30 1892 in Washington D. C., Fletcher told the reporters and old soldiers,

> *I know all you old fellows. I'm here having a good time. I'm meeting the old soldiers and they are having a good time spinning yarns. An old soldier telling his experiences always remind me of the man who was always telling his wife and daughter what he had done in the war. He had done wonders. Finally, one day his daughter said to his wife: 'Mamma, why didn't Mr. Lincoln help papa put down the rebellion?' Don't tell them I said so, but these old soldiers are the biggest liars in creation. Some time when I have time I'll tell you what I did. I served under General Frank Blair, and he was one of the best, biggest-hearted, true soldiers I have ever met. He served his God and his country as only such a man could. And the boys under him were true blue too. Boys, this country belongs to us. Yes, it does, for if it had not been for us it would not exist now.*[315]

Newspaper Banner, 1892; Public Domain.

Much of Fletcher's business efforts continued to center on influencing government officials in some manner or another. In early 1890 he

---

[315] *Sedalia Democrat* (Sedalia, Missouri), September 30, 1892, 10.

successfully got a bill passed in the House that protected the government from under-capitalized railroad companies that wanted to compete in the Indian Territory.[316] Unscrupulous entrepreneurs attempted to talk their way into obtaining valuable right-of-way's. Fletcher demanded a "good-faith" and refundable deposit before one could even begin to discuss business efforts. In addition to being good policy for the government, it also protected the Native-Americans from being further exploited.

While he had an office on 1339 F street, he frequently visited the Willard Hotel to talk less formally with many officials. President Grant had been known for smoking his cigars in the lobby and meeting with those who would request his assistance.[317] Later presidents and other important officials continued the practice of meeting people outside of their offices. For his first few years in the Capital Fletcher's influence and reputation continued to grow but income continued to be problematic. Cases that were tried before the Supreme Court could be lucrative but laborious. Remuneration could be delayed for months or even years.

By 1893 his finances recovered as a big case settled and the country of Siam (Thailand) contracted with him to represent their interests in Washington. Siam had a serious international crisis on its hands. France considered all of Indochina as in their "sphere of influence." They considered Siam a weak country that happened to be located in their way to consolidation of the area. The nearby French protectorate, Vietnam, claimed part of Siam (Laos) as their territory. Shortly after Siam refuted this claim, a French Man of War sailed into Siam and sent troops to bivouac on Siamese territory. Once settled, the French just occupied their positions daring the Siamese to resist. The Siamese minister, believing that England and/or the United States would help them obtain a diplomatic and legal remedy, retained Thomas C. Fletcher as legal counsel. He was to render an opinion on the point in question and discuss the concern with the U.S. State Department. Siam hoped his relationship with the State Department might use its influence with England to intervene. Fletcher lobbied both formally and informally with

---

[316] *St Louis Post Dispatch,* January 26, 3.

[317] This practice of Grant's is where many people believe the term "lobbying" originated. While not really accurate, it certainly appears to have popularized the term.

the U.S. State Department officials. He also reached out to the president. Fletcher represented Siam as things went from bad to worse.[318] In early Spring, 1893, The French Gunboat, Lutin, sailed into Bangkok harbor—essentially blockading the port and escalating hostilities. A brief war ensued that severed parts of Siam and enriched France. Throughout the conflict, Fletcher remained Siam's legal counsel in the United States. The war ended in October, 1893, with terms mostly amicable to the French. Siam lost Laos and other rights and had to pay indemnities. It could have been much worse. Had not England assisted in the final negotiations, Siam's sovereignty would have been severely compromised.

The other parts of his practice continued to do well and there was even consideration of him for an under-secretary position in Treasury, as Secretary of Indian Affairs or Commissioner of Pensions. In 1897, The *St. Louis Post Dispatch* noted of Fletcher at the time that he was a "...*hale and vigorous man of commanding presence.*"[319] While complimentary, it wasn't quite true. The *commanding pres*ence still existed, but his health began to slide downward. He had also lost his older brother, John William (*called* "*J.W.*"), who had died in May of 1894 at the age of 79. The Fletchers had always been a close family but Colonel J. W. Fletcher had been somewhat of a rebel and a hero to the younger siblings. He had reveled in telling Tom, his impressionable younger brother by almost nine years, about his life while being a "49er in California and other adventures. During the Civil War Tom surpassed him in rank and fame, but they remained as close as the age gap and distance would allow. J. W.'s later life in De Soto after the Civil War had not been quite as exciting as his younger brother's but he had still been important to the local community and a substantial land-holder. Few of Tom's extended family remained. He held close to Clara as they lived so far away from those remaining family members. Tom and Clara still took their treasured evening walks near their home; weather permitting.

By the national Republican ascendency in 1896, Tom's practice had slowed down substantially. He probably felt good about the election of

---

[318] *The Sioux County Herald,* (Sioux County, Iowa), May 3, 1893, 2.
[319] *St. Louis Post-Dispatch*, Mar 28, 1897, 3.

William McKinley and his boisterous vice-president, Theodore Roosevelt. Fletcher attempted to secure a position as Register of the Treasure shortly after the election. In April, 1897, a Philadelphia newspaper, noted about Fletcher, "*He was a soldier in the Union Army and was a trusted general officer with Sherman in his March Through Georgia. He is venerable and honorable and his chances are very good. He saw the president today.*"[320] While dozens of newspapers across the region touted his qualifications, he did not get the job.

Regardless of his lack of success in obtaining the federal position, he remained in the public eye. In his many formal and informal encounters with friends in government, Tom continued to discuss the events which shaped the nation's destiny. The Klondike Gold Rush in 1897 likely brought memories of his big brother's adventure. And, the Spanish-American War surely worried him. Tom had frequent opportunities to be away from home in his interactions with political and business leaders. But, not many of his meetings were profitable. He successfully sponsored a fellow member of the Loyal Legion to practice before the U.S. Supreme Court.[321] He gave speeches to the National Republican Club, assisted with the inaugural parade plans for McKinley, and assisted in the procurement of statues of Thomas Hart Benton and Frank Blair for the U.S. Capitol among other activities. Of course, he still practiced before the Supreme Court and facilitated petitioners to obtain federal positions. And, he and Clara took walks each evening as they could.

The winter of 1898-1899 had been

ALL HOPE ABANDONED.

EX-GOV. FLETCHER'S DEATH A QUESTION OF A FEW HOURS.

A special telegram from Washington to the Post-Dispatch Tuesday noon states that Dr. Babbitt, who is attending former Gov. Thomas C. Fletcher, recently stricken

EX-GOV. THOMAS C. FLETCHER.

Death Announcement that ran in hundreds of papers; Public Domain.

---

[320] *The Times* (Philadelphia, Pennsylvania), April 1, 1897, 4.

[321] *Evening Star,* May 4, 1896, 2.

particularly difficult. As he aged, the cold seemed to reach into his very core. And, he had been alone after the first of the year as Clara went to St. Louis to spend some time with Ella. Washington D.C. was an expensive place to live and his finances were not as lush as he had hoped for. While still a practicing lawyer, even before the U.S. Supreme Court, the cases seemed to come less frequently. And, when he walked the halls of the Capital, the faces he passed were increasingly unfamiliar. The "Man to go to from Missouri" had become more and more irrelevant. Perhaps the loss of the Federal position as Register of the Treasury weighed on him. It would have assured a satisfactory income. With personal finances questionable, he contracted with a patent medicine company for the use of his portrait in their marketing. Pe-ru-na actually consisted primarily of two-thirds water, a little flavoring, burnt-caramel coloring and one-third alcohol. Fletcher might have turned to it for some relief on cold winter nights. Probably opportunistically, his image began to be seen in newspapers shortly after his death.

On February 21, 1899, Fletcher had an early appointment at the famous Willard Hotel where he had frequently met with President Ulysses Grant, General William T. Sherman, Cabinet Secretaries, Financial tycoons, lobbyists, and many of the "movers and shakers" of the day. The frigid month of February had already stressed the population. Temperatures had reached near or below zero continuously for the three weeks before this monumental day. Snow still blanketed the city streets and sidewalks. Tom likely felt getting out in this kind of weather would be worth his efforts. Facing the harsh winter conditions must have taxed his physical health as the cold penetrated his chest. But, he probably looked to represent a new client that could bring him needed lucrative fees. But, that would not happen. Just a few feet inside lobby Tom Fletcher, as he brushed the snow off his coat and stamped his feet to remove slush, he realized something was wrong—very wrong. He suddenly clutched his chest and slowly dropped to the floor in pain—great pain.

Later that day, Fletcher's hometown paper, *The St. Louis Post Dispatch*, announced that he had suffered apoplexy while in the lobby of the Willard Hotel in Washington D.C. but was resting comfortably. It noted that his wife had been visiting their daughter at 2646 Lafayette Ave in St. Louis but had departed for Washington to be with her husband.[322]

Clara arrived in time to spend the next several weeks with her dying husband. Her daughter, Ella, came in time to be with her mother later in the vigil. On March 25, 1899, Ex-governor Thomas C. Fletcher died as his wife, daughter and Doctor Babbitt, his personal physician, sat by his side.[323] His remains were returned to St. Louis and were buried two days later in Bellefontaine Cemetery. Ex-governors Francis and Stone, ex-Lieutenant-Governors E. O. Standard, John T. O'Meara, Charles P. Johnson and R. A. Campbell served as pallbearers.

But his story did not end; at least for a while. For several weeks hundreds of newspapers all across the nation carried biographies and memorials to him. Most placed the story of Thomas C. Fletcher on the front page whether it was carried in New Orleans, New York, Cincinnati, Kansas City, Iowa, Omaha, Little Rock, Sacramento, Washington D.C., or other areas. The ex-governor of Missouri still drew an incredible amount of national attention—even in death.

The Loyal Legion, a little over two years later erected a monument in Bellefontaine cemetery. It was made of Missouri Granite six and one-half feet high.

Thomas C. Fletcher,
Born 1827 Died 1899
Brevet Brigadier-General, U. S. V.,
January 1865
Governor of the State
of Missouri
1865-1869[324]

---

[322] *St. Louis Post-Dispatch,* February 21, 1899, 8.

[323] Clara lived with her daughter in St. Louis until her death in 1907 remaining active in the DAR, WCTU, Episcopal Church, veterans' and social organizations.

[324] *St. Louis Post-Dispatch* (St. Louis, Missouri), June 13, 1901, 9.

Clara Fletcher participated in the dedication. The group sang *"America,"* and *"Tenting on the Old Camp Ground."* George S. Grover, a former Captain during the Civil War and a prominent attorney for the Wabash Railroad, made the address at the dedication of the memorial to Governor Fletcher,

> We meet today to unveil a monument to one of our beloved and departed companions, who was as well a commanding and historic figure in the nation, and in his native state, Missouri, in the heroic time when the destiny of this great commonwealth was forever settled on the side of freedom....
>
> ...He was the friend and confidant of President Lincoln, from 1860 until the untimely ending of the life of that greatest American Statesman....
>
> Col. Fletcher was a born soldier, as well as a leader of men, and though a strict disciplinarian, was beloved by all who ever served with him because he shared every hardship with his men, led them gallantly against the enemy in every action and was generous and thoughtful as he was inflexibly just....
>
> ...He was the first republican and first native Missourian elected governor of the state. It is safe to say the State never had a better executive officer.... the verdict of history is and will be, that the foundation of the present greatness of Missouri was laid during the administration of Gen. Thomas C. Fletcher....
>
> The returning ex-confederate soldiers of Missouri never had at any time a better friend than Governor Fletcher....
>
> Early in life he became a member of the Methodist church and lived and died in that faith. Gen. Fletcher was of commanding presence, a very handsome man, with great personal magnetism and winning address. Everyone who knew him loved him. He was generous to a fault, incapable of malice, and was never know in all his life to utter an unkind

word against anyone, whether friend or foe…we will live in
the hope of meeting him again, never to part, on the far side
of the "Shining River.[325]

After Clara lost her husband, she continued remained active in the community and eventually opened a boarding home at 2841 Russell Avenue in St. Louis. She died in 1907 at the age of eighty. He daughter Ella's husband served as the treasurer of the 1904 World's Fair but he died just before it opened. Ella became the *"Hostess of the Fair"* and became an attendant at the St. Louis Art Museum serving until she died in 1928. Ella's brother moved into his mother's boarding house, continued to work as a civil engineer until his death in the late 1920's. Each of these family members along with Ella's husband, Perry were eventually interred at the grave site in the Bellefontaine cemetery. Their respective names were inscribed on the side of Tom's monument. With their respective deaths, the direct line from the famous Missourian ended.

Within twenty years of Thomas C. Fletcher's death, this remarkable Missourian and famous Governor had mostly been forgotten. After fifty years had passed, Fletcher had been totally "lost" to history. He became a minor "footnote" in the story of the state. The reasons for this can be debated. Perhaps, the change in Missouri administrations from Republican to Democrat could have influenced the later public perceptions of his life. Perhaps, Fletcher's dedication to minority rights might have frowned upon by many white leaders and historians of the late nineteenth and twentieth centuries. Perhaps, Missourians stopped "looking backward" for answers to pending issues. Perhaps, because he did not hold any national office or commit any atrocity his name faded into obscurity. Regardless, he has been lost to Missourians.

Recognizing this book's limitations, its publication is intended to help Missouri "rediscover" Thomas C. Fletcher. It is hoped that the book provides a compelling "skeleton" of the man's life. This work can be used by future historians who might be interested enough to "flesh-it-out" and bring his story to life.

---

[325] George S. Grover, Address at Bellefontaine Cemetery, June 12, 1901, Missouri Historical Society, Fletcher Collection.

List of Accomplishments

Thomas C. Fletcher, for all his accomplishments, shortly after his death became the *"Lost Governor"* in Missouri history. A review by the author of twenty text-books and other books about Missouri History found these three things were often said and usually no more: 1) he was the last Civil War Governor; 2) he was the first Republican governor of Missouri; 3) he opposed the Drake Constitution. Some books only report his election and say nothing more about him.

In addition to these, perhaps more could be said:

1. He was the first native-born Missouri Governor
2. He led the anti-slavery party members into the Republican Party before the Civil War
3. He served his country with distinction:
    a. Fought to free slaves
    b. Wounded in action
    c. P.O.W.
    d. Hero of Battle of Pilot Knob
    e. Respected by his men
4. He enforced the law as governor; regardless of his personal feelings

5. He welcomed back former rebels and advocated for reconciliation
6. He welcomed and supported black Missourians
    a. Enrolled them into the Militia
    b. Assisted in the development of educational opportunities for them
    c. Advocated for their equality
7. He was the first president and founding trustee of Lincoln Institute, later Lincoln University (the first black college west of the Mississippi)
8. He supported increases in education across the state for all citizens
9. His administration significantly reduced the state debt
10. He stabilized and caused the growth of the rail system in Missouri
11. He led the successful efforts to restore law and order to the Missouri after the war
12. He stabilized the election process in Missouri
13. He led the successful attempt to increase agricultural production in Missouri
    a. Introduction of new farming techniques
    b. Protection of cattle herds
    c. Addition of new farms and farm land
14. He led the successful efforts to increase Missouri's population
    a. Created immigration department in the state government
    b. Encouraged counties to develop outreach efforts
    c. Personally traveled to the northeast states to recruit immigrants
15. He successfully aided national Veterans' organizations in regard to
    a. Soldiers' homes
    b. Veterans' benefits
    c. Recognition of Veterans' service
16. He led investigations that improved conditions on Indian reservations and advocated for fair treatment
    a. Red Cloud Agency
    b. Cherokee Strip
    c. Many others

17. He successfully represented clients before circuit, district, appellate, and the U.S. Supreme Court
18. He represented Siam's interests in the United States
19. He lobbied for his clients in Congress, among the Departments and with presidents
20. He led the initial delegation to the U.S. Congress which became the first step in St. Louis becoming the home to the World's Fair in 1904

Thomas C. Fletcher has not only been forgotten; he has been underestimated. No other Missouri Governor has ever faced the challenges he confronted. Not only did he confront them, he overcame them and set the stage for future state development. In his time, it was thought that the foundation of the greatness of Missouri was laid during the administration of Thomas C. Fletcher. But he was much more. After serving as governor, Thomas C. Fletcher continued to serve his state and his nation and to live his life with grace and integrity. There is much to learn from looking at his life—even today; maybe especially today.

Bibliography

Primary Sources

"Admission Card to the Fifteenth Banquet of the Society of the Army of Tennessee," Missouri History Museum Archives, St. Louis.

"Articles of Incorporation [Lincoln University]. Jefferson City, Missouri. Lincoln University Archives.

Bench and Bar, St. Louis, KC, Jefferson City, Missouri Historical Society Archives, Reading Room, 282.

Campbell, Hugh to Michael Williams, March 23, 1866, 1866 Letterbook, Mercantile Library, St. Louis, Missouri

Campbell, Robert to Thomas Fletcher, March 1, 1866; 1866 Letterbook, Mercantile Library, St. Louis, Missouri

Campbell, Robert to J.J. Crittenden, January 14, 1861, Letterbook, Mercantile Library, St. Louis, Missouri

Cavada, F.F. *Experiences of a Prisoner of War in Richmond, VA, 1863-64.* Philadelphia, Pennsylvania. King and Baird, 1864

Dyer, Fredrick H. "A Compendium of the War of the Rebellion, V.III," Des Moines, Iowa. Dyer Publishing Company. 1908.

"Thomas Fletcher, Governor of Missouri." *Ladies' Repository.* Cincinnati, Ohio, 1868.

Fletcher, Thomas C. Executive Order of Governor Thomas C. Fletcher, January 6, 1865, Missouri Historical Society Archives, St. Louis, Missouri.

Fletcher, Thomas C., *Harper's Magazine,* June 6, 1863, 362-363.

Fletcher, Thomas. Letter to Colonel, June 22, 1863. Missouri Historical Society Fletcher Collection.

Fletcher, Thomas C. 1891 Letter to Irwin Z. Smith. St. Louis, Missouri. Missouri Historical Museum Archives. Civil War Collection.

Fletcher, Thomas. Letter to the President, October 6, 1868, Missouri Historical Society. Fletcher Collection.

Fletcher, Thomas C. *Life and Reminiscences of General Wm. T. Sherman,* (Baltimore, Maryland). R. H. Woodward Co. 1891.

Fletcher, Thomas C. "Missouri's Jubilee." Jefferson City, Missouri. W.A Curry, Public Printer. 1865.

"The Founding of Lincoln University." Jefferson City, Missouri. Lincoln University Archives.

Frizzel, Williard. Personal Papers, Missouri History Museum Archives, St. Louis.

1870 Gould's City Directory, St. Louis, Missouri. Missouri Historical Society, 1870.

Grant, U.S. *Personal Memoirs, Vol.* I, New York, New York. Charles L. Webster & Company 1885.

Grover, George S. Address at Bellefontaine Cemetery. June 12, 1901. Missouri Historical Society, Fletcher Collection.

"Harrisonville Monroe County, Illinois." extracted from *Combined History of Randolph, Monroe and Perry Counties, Illinois.* Philadelphia, Pennsylvania. J. L. McDonough & Co.1883.

"Historical and Biographical Notes." Finding Aid 3.18. Jefferson City, Missouri. Missouri State Archives.

Jefferson County Court Records, 1830-1865. Hillsboro Court House. Hillsboro, Missouri. "Jefferson County Towns and Villages." *GOODSPEED's HISTORY OF Franklin, Jefferson, Washington, Crawford, & Gasconade Counties, Missouri.* Chicago, Illinois. The Goodspeed Publishing Co.1888.

Kremer, *Gary R. James Milton Turner and the Promise of America.* Columbia, Illinois, University of Missouri Press, 1991

Parker, Nathan H. *Handbook: The State of Missouri,* Governor's Inaugural, St. Louis, Missouri. P. M. Pinckard. 1865.

Petition, Civil War Collection St. Louis, Missouri. Missouri History Museum.

Pollard, Edward. *Southern History of the War* New York, New York. C.B. Richardson.1866.

"Records of the Field Office for the State of Missouri, Bureau of Refugees, Freedmen, and Abandoned Lands (Freedmen's Bureau) for Missouri, 1865–1872.

Schuchert, Charles. "Biographical Memoir of Othneil Charles Marsh, 1831-1899. Presentation to the Academy at the Annual Meeting. 1938. 13.

Snead, Thomas L. *The Fight for Missouri* New York, New York. Charles Scribner's Sons. 1886.

Newspapers

Abilene Daily Reflector (Abilene, Kansas). January 25, 1889.

Albany Ledger (Albany, Missouri). March 31, 1899.

Alexandria Gazette, (Alexandria, Virginia). October 7, 1865.

Arkansas City Daily Traveler (Arkansas City, Kansas). October 9, 1894.

Atchison Daily Champion (Atchison, Kansas). 1867-1875.

Baltimore Sun (Baltimore, Maryland), 1871-1878.

Boon's Lick Times (Fayette, Missouri), February 4, 1843.

Chicago Tribune (Chicago, Illinois). 1864-1877.

The Courier-Journal (Louisville, Kentucky), September 24, 1866.

The Daily Journal (Wilmington, North Carolina), September 6, 1866.

Daily Ohio Statesman (Columbus, Ohio), December 22, 1866.

Detroit Free Press (Detroit, Michigan), March 21, 1863-1866.

Evening Star (Washington D.C.), 1889-1890.

The Fremont Weekly Journal (Fremont, Ohio), May 8, 1863.

Fort Scott Weekly Monitor (Fort Scott, Kansas), August 19, 1868.

The Glasgow Weekly Times (Glascow, Missouri), 1856-1861.

Harper's Weekly (New York, New York), 1862-1865.

Harrisburg Telegraph (Harrisburg, Pennsylvania), 1866-1867.

Hartford Courant (Hartford, Connecticut), November 16, 1866.

Holt County Sentinel (Oregon, Missouri), 1865-1896.

The Howard Union (Glasgow, Missouri), 1865-1872.

The Inter Ocean (Chicago, Illinois), 1872-1875.

Ironton County Register (Ironton, Missouri), January 14, 1892.

Liberty Tribune (Liberty, Missouri), December 14, 1860.

The Lincoln County Herald (Troy, Missouri), November 3, 1870.

The Louisville Daily Courier (Louisville, Kentucky), December 14, 1866. 4.

Missouri Republican (St. Louis, Missouri), May 9, 1846-1861.

Missouri State Times (Jefferson City, Missouri), 1865.

Muskogee Phoenix (Muskogee, Oklahoma), May 22, 1890.

Nashville Union and American (Nashville, Tennessee), January 12, 1869.

National Republican (Washington, District of Columbia), February 8, 1870.

Nebraska State Journal (Lincoln, Nebraska), October 1, 1875, 2.

New York Daily Herald (New York, New York), 1875-1878.

Palmyra Weekly Whig (Palmyra, Missouri), September 16, 1847.

Philadelphia Enquirer (Philadelphia, Pennsylvania), April 6, 1865.

The Pittsburgh Daily Commercial (Pittsburgh, Pennsylvania), March 9, 1865.

Pittsburgh Daily Post (Pittsburgh, Pennsylvania), 1889-1890.

Pittsburg Dispatch (Pittsburgh, Pennsylvania) July 15, 1889.

The Plymouth Democrat (Plymouth, Indiana)., September 12, 1867.

The Radical (Bowling Green, Missouri), January 11, 1845.

Richmond Dispatch (Richmond, Virginia), May 8, 1863-1869.

St. Joseph Free Weekly Democrat March 17, 1860.

St. Louis Post-Dispatch (St. Louis, Missouri), 1865-1907.

The St. Louis Star and Times (St. Louis, Missouri), February 12, 1934.

Sedalia Democrat (Sedalia, Missouri), September 30, 1892.

The Sioux County Herald (Sioux County, Iowa), May 3, 1893.

Staunton Spectator (Staunton, Virginia), August 14, 18.

The Southern Standard (Arkadelphia, Arkansas), July 21, 1883.

The Times (Philadelphia Pennsylvania), April 1, 1897, 4.

The Titusville Herald (Titusville, Pennsylvania), December 1, 1870.

The Topeka Daily Capital (Topeka, Kansas), April 4, 1885.

Warrenton Banner (Warrenton, Missouri), 1869-1870.

Washington Post (Washington D. C.) December 21, 1890.

Washington Telegraph (Washington, Arkansas) July 5, 1865.

Weekly Arkansas Gazette (Little Rock, Arkansas), 1865-1867.

The Weekly Caucasian (Lexington, Missouri), March 5, 1868-1870.

Wichita Daily Eagle (Wichita, Kansas), June 14, 1880.

Books and Pamphlets

Barnes. Harper. *Standing on a Volcano: The Life and Times of David Rowland Francis.* St. Louis. Missouri Historical Society Press. 2001.

Brands, H.W. *The Man Who Saved the Union; Ulysses Grant in War and Peace.* New York, New York. Doubleday. 2012.

Byrd Family History, unpublished by Betty Vinyard, Jefferson County, Missouri, 2007.

De Soto Historical Society. *De Soto, Missouri: A Pictorial History.* Self-published, no. date.

Giffen, Jerena East Giffen. *First Ladies of Missouri.* Jefferson City, Missouri. Wadsworth Publishing Co. 1996.

Hallemann, Dave. *Hallemann's Interpretation of the 1876 Historical Atlas.* Self-published, 1998.

Hoelzel, Norma. *De Soto, Missouri Bicentennial, 1803-2003.* Bicentennial Committee, 2003.

The Life and Times of Thomas Clement Fletcher, Jefferson County, Missouri. Jefferson Heritage and Landmark Society. 1994.

McLachlan, Sean. McLachlan. *It Happened in Missouri,* Hartford, Connecticut. Morris B Book Publishing Co, Globe Pequot Press. 2008.

Meyer, Duane G. *The Heritage of Missouri.* St. Louis, Missouri. River City Publishers. 1982.

Miller, Eddie. *As You Were: A History of De Soto and Surrounding Area.* *Series published in De Soto Press* (De Soto, Missouri). 1968-1971.

Nagel, Paul. *Missouri: A History.* New York, New York. W.W. Norton & Company. 1977.

Parish, William E. Parrish. *A History of Missouri, Vol. III.* Columbia, Missouri. University of Missouri Press, 2001

Parish, William E. Parish. *Missouri Under Radical Rule, 1865-1870.* Columbia, Missouri. University of Missouri Press. 1965.

Pechmann, Oliver R. *The Hero from Jefferson County: Thomas Clement Fletcher.* Self-published. 2016.

Peterson, Cyrus A. and Joseph M. Hanson. *The Battle of Pilot Knob.* Independence, Missouri. Two Trails Publishing. 2000.

Primm, James Neal. *Lion of the Valley,* Bolder Colorado. Pruett Publishing Company. 1981.

Rutledge, Zoe Booth. *Our Jefferson County Heritage,* St. Louis, Missouri. Ramfre Press. 1973

Schultz, Duane. *Quantrill's War.* New York, New York. St Martin's Griffin. 1996.

Tebbel, John. *The Compact History of the Indian Wars.* New York, New York. Tower Publications, Inc. 1966.

Trefousse, Hans Louis. *Andrew Johnson.* New York, New York. W.W. Norton & Company. 1997.

Vexler, Robert I. *St. Louis: A Chronological and Documentary History.* Dobbes Ferry, New York. Oceana Publications, Inc. 1974.

Thesis/Dissertation unpublished

Gildner, Major Gray M. "The Chickasaw Bayou Campaign." U.S. Army and General Staff College, Fort Leavenworth, Kansas, M.A. 1991.

Hawver, Marlene. "Robert Campbell, Expectant Capitalist." University of Nebraska, MA. 1983.

Huss, Stephen Huss. *Take No Advantage.* St. Louis, Missouri. St. Louis University. Ph.D. 1989.

Internet

Mike Allard, "Army of Tennessee." Mississippi Civil War Message Board. *http. Mississippi, Civil War Message Board.*

Election of 1856. www.Wikipidia.org.

Gathman, Allen. "Missouri Convention Rejects Secession." March 19, 2011. *http://gathkinsons.net/sesqui/?p-2265.*

Mills, Major Milton, Personal Papers of Major Milton Mills, 16th OVI Letter from Benjamin Heckert Description of Battle of Chickasaw Bayou December 21, 1904. *www.mkwe.co.*

"Isidor Bush, Jewish Pioneer; A Man for All Seasons, St. Louis, Missouri." *www.JMAW.org*

Presidency, *www.UCSB.EDU,* Election of 1856.

Red Cloud Quotes. *www.Firstpeople.us.*

Know Nothing. *www.Wikipedia.org,*

About the Author

D r. Huss holds a Ph.D. in American Studies from St. Louis University, an MA in History from Southeast Missouri State University, and a BSE from the University of Central Arkansas. He served as one of the founders and as the President and Chief Executive Officer of the COMTREA Community Comprehensive Health Center in Jefferson County, Missouri, from 1974 to 2016. Huss taught as an adjunct-instructor in American History for over 20 years at the Jefferson Community  College in Hillsboro. He also has taught World Religions, Western Civilization, and American Politics.

He is a member of the Fletcher House Foundation, the Vice-President of the Jefferson County Heritage and History Society, serves as a Missouri Mental Health Commissioner and served as historian of the Jefferson County Bicentennial Committee providing over fifty presentations on the history of Jefferson County in 2018.

Dr. Huss has presented over 200 workshops to the St. Louis community on topics such as preventing youth violence, alcoholism and other drug abuse prevention, Jefferson County history, teaching children of divorce, motivation in the classroom, Seven Habits of Effective People, management effectiveness, values clarification and stress management. He has published four books and many articles.

He lives just outside of Hillsboro, Missouri, in Jefferson County, with his wife, Dr. Renee A. Huss. His family includes: Michael Huss and wife Misty; Jason Meyers and his wife Katy; Justin Huss and his wife Jennifer; Joshua Meyers and his wife Amy; Rebecca Ashley and her husband, Paul; Geanna Moore and her husband, Tracy; and his twelve grandchildren.

He can be reached at www.sfhuss@gmail.com and welcomes correspondence.